THE
YAKIMA

CANADA

WASHINGTON

River

MONTANA

Columbia

**Coast
Salish**

Spokane

Spokane

River

M
O
U
N
T
A
I
N
S

*Puget
Sound*

Wenatchi

Columbia-Sinkiuse

**Coeur
d'Alene**

Flathead

PACIFIC
OCEAN

Kittitas

Wanapam

Palus

Chinook

Yakima

YAKIMA

Smake

River

Klickitat
Wishham

River

Walla Walla

Columbia   *River*

Umatilla

Nez Percé

Columbia

Warm Springs

Cayuse

C
A
S
C
A
D
E

Willamette   River

IDAHO

OREGON

Shoshone

THE
YAKIMA

Helen H. Schuster
Iowa State University

Frank W. Porter III
General Editor

CHELSEA HOUSE PUBLISHERS
New York   Philadelphia

On the cover   A 20th-century Yakima basketry hat.

Chelsea House Publishers
Editor-in-Chief Nancy Toff
Executive Editor Remmel T. Nunn
Managing Editor Karyn Gullen Browne
Copy Chief Juliann Barbato
Picture Editor Adrian G. Allen
Art Director Maria Epes
Manufacturing Manager Gerald Levine

Indians of North America
Senior Editor Liz Sonneborn

Staff for **THE YAKIMA**
Associate Editor Will Broaddus
Copy Editor Philip Koslow
Editorial Assistant Nicole Claro
Assistant Art Director Loraine Machlin
Designer Donna Sinisgalli
Assistant Designer James Baker
Picture Researcher Michèle Brisson
Production Manager Joseph Romano
Production Coordinator Marie Claire Cebrián

First Printing

1 3 5 7 9 8 6 4 2

Library of Congress Cataloging-in-Publication Data

Schuster, Helen H.
The Yakima/Helen H. Schuster.
   p.   cm.—(Indians of North America)
Includes bibliographical references.
Summary: Examines the culture, history, and changing
fortunes of the Yakima Indians.
ISBN 1-55546-735-0
      0-7910-0402-3 (pbk.)
1. Yakima Indians.   [1. Yakima Indians. 2. Indians of
North America.] I. Title. II. Series: Indians of North America
(Chelsea House Publishers)   89-23903
E99.Y2S38 1990   CIP
973′.04974—dc20   AC

CONTENTS

INDIANS OF NORTH AMERICA

CHELSEA HOUSE PUBLISHERS

INDIANS OF NORTH AMERICA: CONFLICT AND SURVIVAL

Frank W. Porter III

The Indians survived our open intention of wiping them out, and since the tide turned they have even weathered our good intentions toward them, which can be much more deadly.

John Steinbeck
America and Americans

When Europeans first reached the North American continent, they found hundreds of tribes occupying a vast and rich country. The newcomers quickly recognized the wealth of natural resources. They were not, however, so quick or willing to recognize the spiritual, cultural, and intellectual riches of the people they called Indians.

The Indians of North America examines the problems that develop when people with different cultures come together. For American Indians, the consequences of their interaction with non-Indian people have been both productive and tragic. The Europeans believed they had "discovered" a "New World," but their religious bigotry, cultural bias, and materialistic world view kept them from appreciating and understanding the people who lived in it. All too often they attempted to change the way of life of the indigenous people. The Spanish conquistadores wanted the Indians as a source of labor. The Christian missionaries, many of whom were English, viewed them as potential converts. French traders and trappers used the Indians as a means to obtain pelts. As Francis Parkman, the 19th-century historian, stated, "Spanish civilization crushed the Indian; English civilization scorned and neglected him; French civilization embraced and cherished him."

Nearly 500 years later, many people think of American Indians as curious vestiges of a distant past, waging a futile war to survive in a Space Age society. Even today, our understanding of the history and culture of American Indians is too often derived from unsympathetic, culturally biased, and inaccurate reports. The American Indian, described and portrayed in thousands of movies, television programs, books, articles, and government studies, has either been raised to the status of the "noble savage" or disparaged as the "wild Indian" who resisted the westward expansion of the American frontier.

Where in this popular view are the real Indians, the human beings and communities whose ancestors can be traced back to ice-age hunters? Where are the creative and indomitable people whose sophisticated technologies used the natural resources to ensure their survival, whose military skill might even have prevented European settlement of North America if not for devastating epidemics and disruption of the ecology? Where are the men and women who are today diligently struggling to assert their legal rights and express once again the value of their heritage?

The various Indian tribes of North America, like people everywhere, have a history that includes population expansion, adaptation to a range of regional environments, trade across wide networks, internal strife, and warfare. This was the reality. Europeans justified their conquests, however, by creating a mythical image of the New World and its native people. In this myth, the New World was a virgin land, waiting for the Europeans. The arrival of Christopher Columbus ended a timeless primitiveness for the original inhabitants.

Also part of this myth was the debate over the origins of the American Indians. Fantastic and diverse answers were proposed by the early explorers, missionairies, and settlers. Some thought that the Indians were descended from the Ten Lost Tribes of Israel, others that they were descended from inhabitants of the lost continent of Atlantis. One writer suggested that the Indians had reached North America in another Noah's ark.

A later myth, perpetrated by many historians, focused on the relentless persecution during the past five centuries until only a scattering of these "primitive" people remained to be herded onto reservations. This view fails to chronicle the overt and covert ways in which the Indians successfully coped with the intruders.

All of these myths presented one-sided interpretations that ignored the complexity of European and American events and policies. All left serious questions unanswered. What were the origins of the American Indians? Where did they come from? How and when did they get to the New World? What was their life—their culture—really like?

In the late 1800s, anthropologists and archaeologists in the Smithsonian Institution's newly created Bureau of American Ethnology in Washington,

8

D.C., began to study scientifically the history and culture of the Indians of North America. They were motivated by an honest belief that the Indians were on the verge of extinction and that along with them would vanish their languages, religious beliefs, technology, myths, and legends. These men and women went out to visit, study, and record data from as many Indian communities as possible before this information was forever lost.

By this time there was a new myth in the national consciousness. American Indians existed as figures in the American past. They had performed a historical mission. They had challenged white settlers who trekked across the continent. Once conquered, however, they were supposed to accept graciously the way of life of their conquerors.

The reality again was different. American Indians resisted both actively and passively. They refused to lose their unique identity, to be assimilated into white society. Many whites viewed the Indians not only as members of a conquered nation but also as "inferior" and "unequal." The rights of the Indians could be expanded, contracted, or modified as the conquerors saw fit. In every generation, white society asked itself what to do with the American Indians. Their answers have resulted in the twists and turns of federal Indian policy.

There were two general approaches. One way was to raise the Indians to a "higher level" by "civilizing" them. Zealous missionaries considered it their Christian duty to elevate the Indian through conversion and scanty education. The other approach was to ignore the Indians until they disappeared under pressure from the ever-expanding white society. The myth of the "vanishing Indian" gave stronger support to the latter option, helping to justify the taking of the Indians' land.

Prior to the end of the 18th century, there was no national policy on Indians simply because the American nation had not yet come into existence. American Indians similarly did not possess a political or social unity with which to confront the various Europeans. They were not homogeneous. Rather, they were loosely formed bands and tribes, speaking nearly 300 languages and thousands of dialects. The collective identity felt by Indians today is a result of their common experiences of defeat and/or mistreatment at the hands of whites.

During the colonial period, the British crown did not have a coordinated policy toward the Indians of North America. Specific tribes (most notably the Iroquois and the Cherokee) became military and political pawns used by both the crown and the individual colonies. The success of the American Revolution brought no immediate change. When the United States acquired new territory from France and Mexico in the early 19th century, the federal government wanted to open this land to settlement by homesteaders. But the Indian tribes that lived on this land had signed treaties with European governments assuring their title to the land. Now the United States assumed legal responsibility for honoring these treaties.

At first, President Thomas Jefferson believed that the Louisiana Purchase contained sufficient land for both the Indians and the white population. Within a generation, though, it became clear that the Indians would not be allowed to remain. In the 1830s the federal government began to coerce the eastern tribes to sign treaties agreeing to relinquish their ancestral land and move west of the Mississippi River. Whenever these negotiations failed, President Andrew Jackson used the military to remove the Indians. The southeastern tribes, promised food and transportation during their removal to the West, were instead forced to walk the "Trail of Tears." More than 4,000 men, woman, and children died during this forced march. The "removal policy" was successful in opening the land to homesteaders, but it created enormous hardships for the Indians.

By 1871 most of the tribes in the United States had signed treaties ceding most or all of their ancestral land in exchange for reservations and welfare. The treaty terms were intended to bind both parties for all time. But in the General Allotment Act of 1887, the federal government changed its policy again. Now the goal was to make tribal members into individual landowners and farmers, encouraging their absorption into white society. This policy was advantageous to whites who were eager to acquire Indian land, but it proved disastrous for the Indians. One hundred thirty-eight million acres of reservation land were subdivided into tracts of 160, 80, or as little as 40 acres, and allotted tribe members on an individual basis. Land owned in this way was said to have "trust status" and could not be sold. But the surplus land—all Indian land not allotted to individuals—was opened (for sale) to white settlers. Ultimately, more than 90 million acres of land were taken from the Indians by legal and illegal means.

The resulting loss of land was a catastrophe for the Indians. It was necessary to make it illegal for Indians to sell their land to non-Indians. The Indian Reorganization Act of 1934 officially ended the allotment period. Tribes that voted to accept the provisions of this act were reorganized, and an effort was made to purchase land within preexisting reservations to restore an adequate land base.

Ten years later, in 1944, federal Indian policy again shifted. Now the federal government wanted to get out of the "Indian business." In 1953 an act of Congress named specific tribes whose trust status was to be ended "at the earliest possible time." This new law enabled the United States to end unilaterally, whether the Indians wished it or not, the special status that protected the land in Indian tribal reservations. In the 1950s federal Indian policy was to transfer federal responsibility and jurisdiction to state governments, encourage the physical relocation of Indian peoples from reservations to urban areas, and hasten the termination, or extinction, of tribes.

Between 1954 and 1962 Congress passed specific laws authorizing the termination of more than 100 tribal groups. The stated purpose of the termination policy was to ensure the full and complete integration of Indians into American society. However, there is a less benign way to interpret this legislation. Even as termination was being discussed in Congress, 133 separate bills were introduced to permit the transfer of trust land ownership from Indians to non-Indians.

With the Johnson administration in the 1960s the federal government began to reject termination. In the 1970s yet another Indian policy emerged. Known as "self-determination," it favored keeping the protective role of the federal government while increasing tribal participation in, and control of, important areas of local government. In 1983 President Reagan, in a policy statement on Indian affairs, restated the unique "government is government" relationship of the United States with the Indians. However, federal programs since then have moved toward transferring Indian affairs to individual states, which have long desired to gain control of Indian land and resources.

As long as American Indians retain power, land, and resources that are coveted by the states and the federal government, there will continue to be a "clash of cultures," and the issues will be contested in the courts, Congress, the White House, and even in the international human rights community. To give all Americans a greater comprehension of the issues and conflicts involving American Indians today is a major goal of this series. These issues are not easily understood, nor can these conflicts be readily resolved. The study of North American Indian history and culture is a necessary and important step toward that comprehension. All Americans must learn the history of the relations between the Indians and the federal government, recognize the unique legal status of the Indians, and understand the heritage and cultures of the Indians of North America.

A Yakima elder and child, photographed in the 1930s. For centuries, the Yakima have passed their traditions from one generation to the next by telling legends.

THE WAY
IT WAS

In the beginning, our Creator spoke the word and this earth was created. He spoke the word again and all living things were put on earth. And then he said the word and we, the [Indian] people, were created and planted here on this earth.

We are like the plants on this earth. Our food was put here as plants to feed us: just like when we plant a garden. That is the way our earth was in the beginning.

There were salmon, deer, elk, and all kinds of birds. It is as if our bodies are the very end of this earth, still growing while our ancestors are all buried in the ground.

He named everything he created. He put water on this earth. He made it flow into the rivers and lakes to water this great garden and to quench the thirst of the people, the animals, plants, birds and fish.

He took the feet of the people and made them walk on this earth. He created the horse; which is like a human being. He put the horse and the people together to help one another.

All of the land where we live and where our ancestors lived was created for the [Indian] people.
—Excerpted from *The Way It Was: Anaku Iwacha, Yakima Indian Legends* by Virginia Beavert.

This legend of the beginning of the world has been told by the Yakima Indians for centuries. The Yakima Indians and their ancestors have always lived along the western part of the great Columbia Plateau in what is now south-central Washington State. The relative isolation of this part of the Plateau long shielded the Yakima and their neigh-

A contemporary photograph of the Yakima River, which runs through the center of the Yakima's homeland. The rich natural resources of the region allowed its prehistoric inhabitants to prosper.

bors from outsiders, enabling them to maintain essentially the same way of life for almost 12,000 years. Of course, as the climate and natural environment changed over this long period, the people developed new technologies and adopted new cultural practices. But many of their traditions survived throughout this time and are observed by the Yakima today.

The Yakima, like most other American Indian societies, have preserved their values and beliefs by passing on knowledge of them orally through their ancient tales. During the cold months of winter, grandparents traditionally recounted these stories to their grandchildren. Seated around a central fire in

a warm winter lodge, the children surrounded the elder storyteller, who always began with the resounding phrase, "Awacha nay!", meaning, "This is the way it was in the legendary days of the animal world!" And the children responded, "Eeee!", which meant, "Yes, we hear; we are listening."

Most Yakima legends depict an age before humans existed, when animals thought and acted like people do now. These animals also had extraordinary powers that they used to prepare the earth for humankind. Many legends tell of Speelyáy (also known as Coyote), a mischievous trickster whose plans and schemes sometimes greatly benefited the world. Sometimes, however, Speel-yáy's plans went astray and he ended up a victim of his own scheming.

Although the tales take place in a mythic age, they say a good deal about the world as the Yakima's ancestors knew it and how it came to be as it is today. The legends explain the origins of landmarks and other natural features in the Yakima homeland, as well as the beginnings of traditional Yakima beliefs. The stories therefore perform the vital function of enabling Yakima children to understand the world they live in, what to expect from it, and how they must behave. This knowledge is especially important in helping Yakima children today maintain their unique identity as the descendants of an ancient people in the modern world.

Although the legends of the early Yakima sometimes differ with more sci-entific sources of information about these people, linguists—scholars of human language—have learned a great deal by collecting and studying their stories. For instance, no Yakima legends tell of migrations of their ancestors to the Columbia Plateau from another area, and their most venerable myths all take place near natural landmarks in what is now Washington State. These facts imply that Yakima country was indeed inhabited for a very long time, probably by the ancestral people of the Yakima and related tribes.

Human beings' long occupation of this region is confirmed by the findings of archaeologists—scholars who study physical evidence of past human societies. Archaeologists have found evidence that people were living here about 12,000 years ago. They have also identified many prehistoric seasonal

Salmon caught in the Yakima and Columbia rivers were a staple of the diet of the Yakima's ancestors.

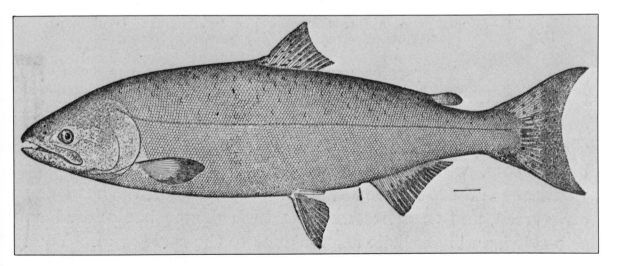

living sites in caves, rock-shelters, and camps scattered throughout the area.

The rich environment of the Yakima homeland allowed prehistoric peoples to prosper there. The Yakima River and its tributaries, one of the major river systems flowing into the Columbia River from the Cascade Mountains to the west, ran through the center of this region. These waterways teemed with salmon, steelhead trout, and other fish. Sacred Mount Adams (or Páhto, meaning "standing high")—a snowcapped giant mountain 12,307 feet in altitude—dominated the entire countryside.

A series of fingerlike ridges, now known as the Yakima Folds, extended into the flat plains of the Yakima River

Sacred Mount Adams, which is known to the Yakima as Páhto (standing high).

valley from the foothills of the mountains. The Yakima River cut a pathway through most of the Yakima Folds on its way to meet the imposing Columbia River, which bisected the entire Columbia Plateau. The Columbia's course ran southward but made a great bend to the west before it finally flowed through the Cascade Mountains to the Pacific Ocean. Legend holds that the original course of the Columbia (which the Yakima called the Enchewána, meaning "the big river") was carved and dug by Wíshpush, a giant beaver. The story states that long ago flood waters covered the region, and the land underneath was revealed only after the waters flowed into the riverbed made by W'ishpush and out to the Pacific Ocean. The beaver therefore helped to prepare the Yakima homeland for human beings.

The Columbia Plateau itself was a semiarid region of open, windswept country that was formed by an ancient lava flow. The territory supported a thin ground cover of sagebrush, juniper, bunchgrass, cheatgrass, and greasewood. Willows, cottonwoods, and tall grasses grew along the streams and rivers. Small animals, such as coyotes, jackrabbits, and various small rodents, abounded throughout the area, and rattlesnakes dominated the canyons and rocky riverbanks. In the spring, migratory birds nested along the streams, and sharp-tailed grouse and sage grouse were found throughout the plains.

Prehistoric artifacts, such as this carved and painted stone effigy found along the Columbia River, attest to the long presence of humans on the Columbia Plateau.

The eastern slopes of the Cascade Mountains were covered with rich forests. Forest wildlife included deer, elks, bears, and a variety of smaller animals, such as beavers, marmots, racoons, and muskrats. At the timberline grew huckleberry bushes, and at lower elevations, nutritious roots were found, such as bitterroot, camas, and wild carrots.

The vegetation and wildlife of the region gave the Yakima's ancestors an abundant supply of food. The earliest people probably relied on hunting deer and elks, as well as mountain sheep and goats, antelope, and bison. However, archaeologists believe that about 5,000 years ago, as the people in the region became more settled, their dependence on wild plants, especially roots and berries, increased.

About 4,500 years ago, the climate of the Columbia Plateau cooled, becoming much as it is today. Temperatures ranged from below 0 degrees Fahrenheit in winter to 100 degrees Fahrenheit in summer. Precipitation was relatively light. There was a moderate amount of snow in winter and rain in spring, but summer and autumn were dry.

At this time, fish became an increasingly large component of the food supply of the Yakima's ancestors. As fishing gained in importance, the number of settlements along the rivers increased. Fishing tools also were developed. These included spears, dipnets, and weirs—structures woven from twigs and sticks that fishermen placed in small streams to trap fish and make them easier to catch.

Archaeologists have found other objects at prehistoric sites in the area that help create a picture of how people lived there long ago. Among these artifacts are stone projectile points for spears and arrows, remains of a decorated wooden bow that was used for hunting, scrapers for skinning and dressing the hides of the animals that hunters killed, woven or coiled basketry fragments, and sewn-rush mats.

The Yakima's ancestors also made digging stick handles from antlers and used mortars and pestles for preparing plant foods. In addition to these functional items, they made wooden combs, shell beads, and carved figurines and bowls from antlers.

More puzzling evidence of prehistoric peoples are the picture writings they left behind. These were carved into the face of tall cliffs along the Columbia River or painted in red, yellow, white, or blue pigments on large rocks along the creeks that feed into the Yakima River. Some depict various game animals, such as bison or mountain sheep. Others may represent mythological figures that are still alive in the legends of the Yakima people. No one knows how old the picture writings are or what they mean. Traditional stories, however, hold that they were made by the Wahtéetas—little people who lived in the cliffs and rocks—and that the pictures contained information about past events and about how people should behave. It is said by the Yakima that it is dangerous for an adult to see a Wahtéeta. But if one appears before a child, it will become the young person's guardian spirit and give him or her protection and special powers.

The Yakima language of ancient times is still spoken today. It is a Northwest Sahaptin dialect of the Sahaptin language, which linguists classify as one of a group of related tongues they call the Sahaptian language family. Sahaptian languages were spoken throughout the southern portion of the

A rock painted with prehistoric picture writing near The Dalles on the Columbia River. Traditional Yakima stories tell that such pictures were drawn by Wahtéetas, *little people who lived in rocks and cliffs.*

Columbia Plateau in the region between the Cascade Mountains and the Bitterroot Mountains in what is now central Idaho. In this area lived various Indian peoples, including the Klikitat, the Wanapam, the Tenino (also known as the Warm Springs), the Walla Walla (Walula), the Umatilla, the Cayuse, and the Nez Percé. Two other languages were spoken on the Plateau. Salish speakers lived to the north and east of the Sahaptian groups; and Upper Chinook speakers lived along the Columbia River just east of the Cascades.

Archaeological records indicate that, despite the language differences, all peoples on the Plateau had essentially similar customs, beliefs, and traditions. They also maintained close ties with one another through intermarriage, trade, visiting, and by sharing hunting, fishing, and root-digging grounds.

However, unlike most of their neighbors, the Yakima today still live on the same land that has been a part of their ancient traditional territory for thousands of years. Their roots are deeply sunk into the earth. Their sense of identity is clear. As a result, many of the Yakima's cherished traditions still live, imparting a sense of the wisdom that sustained the people in the past and enabled them to survive into the present. ▲

A Yakima woman wearing a beaded dress and basketry hat, photographed by Edward S. Curtis in 1910.

THE
TRADITIONAL
YAKIMA WORLD

When Yakima elders today describe their traditional way of life, they usually begin with the English words *long time*. By this, they mean "a long time ago before whites came to our country and changed our way of life—this is the way it used to be."

Long time, the Yakima people probably numbered about 7,000. They lived in 60 to 70 small, independent permanent villages that were usually established along waterways. Families were identified largely by the name of their village, a tradition that continues to this day. The importance of the relationship between the Yakima and their land was expressed by Robert Jim, a noted tribal leader, in an address he made at a ceremonial gathering in 1972: "The land don't belong to the Indian; the Indian belongs to the land!"

The Yakima stayed in their village during the winter. For most of the rest of the year, they lived in smaller, dispersed, temporary camps as they traveled from place to place in search of food, returning to their village when necessary. The Yakima derived their subsistence primarily by fishing and by gathering wild plants, but they supplemented their food supply by hunting. In order to obtain as much food as possible, they traveled to wherever plants or wildlife were most plentiful during a specific time of the year. Although the camps they established at these sites were temporary, they had an air of permanence because people tended to return to the same areas year after year.

When the snows melted in February, the Yakima prepared to depart on their seasonal round of food gathering.

Before leaving their winter village, they waited for the first wild-plant food to appear, a stalk called *khásiya*, meaning "first celery." The Yakima then gathered these stalks and held a first-foods feast to celebrate their bounty.

In late February or March, the people arrived at fishing stations on the Columbia River or on the Yakima River and its tributaries. At this time the rivers teemed with life as many varieties of salmon (*núsukh*)—including chinook, silver, sockeye, and chum—traveled upstream to their spawning grounds. Yakima legend credits Speelyáy, the mischievous trickster, with being responsible for the annual salmon runs. He was said to have broken a dam erected by the Swallow Sisters and thus freed the salmon to swim upstream to the people, who had been starving.

Before Yakima fishermen could catch the salmon, they had to receive their leader's permission to fish. This system allowed some salmon to escape upstream and reproduce and therefore ensured that there would be plenty of fish in future years. Also before general fishing was permitted, several fish were ritually caught by a group of seven men. They then prepared their catch for a first-salmon feast. With this ceremony, the Yakima gave thanks for the renewal of this important food source.

In addition to salmon, the Yakima fished for steelhead trout, sturgeon, suckers, and lampreys. To catch them, they used a variety of tools, including two-pronged harpoons, leisters, gaffs,

seines, spears, weirs, and several types of nets.

The Yakima's principal fisheries on the Columbia River were at Celilo Falls and the Dalles; at Priest Rapids among their close relatives, the Wanapam; and at the great fishery at Wenatshapam in Wenatchi territory. Two to three thousand people would come together to fish at these sites. In 1824, Sir George Simpson of the Hudson's Bay Company wrote that "the shores [of the Columbia] are actually lined with Indian lodges; . . . the whole of the Interior population flock to its banks at the fishing season."

As the number of fish at these sites dwindled in late April, families traveled to favorite root-digging grounds. In these areas, women collected more than 20 varieties of roots. They dug roots using a curved and pointed hardwood stick, about 30 inches long, with a short crosswise handle made of horn or antler. Women pushed their root digger into the ground under a plant and then pulled on the handle to pry the root to the surface. A good root digger was highly prized. They are still used by the Yakima today, but modern root diggers are made from steel.

While women were occupied digging roots and preparing their surplus for storage, men often hunted. Hunters traditionally used bows and arrows to kill elks, bears, wolves, foxes, and mountain sheep and goats. Hunters also stalked game birds. However, the animal most important to the Yakima was the *yámish*, or "deer." In addition to venison, deer provided them with hides. After deer hides were fleshed, scraped, and tanned, the Yakima used them to make clothing, portable shelters, and household equipment.

The Yakima used the bones and antlers of various animals to make tools and tool handles. For instance, the horns of mountain sheep and goats were carved into spoons, ladles, and other utensils.

In June of every year, men left the hunt and women left their root-digging grounds. Families then once again gathered at various fishing sites to intercept the second annual salmon run. The most popular site was the large Wenatshapam fishery, which the Yakima shared with the Wenatchi Indians to the north. In July, families moved to higher elevations in the mountains to escape the heat. There men hunted and women gathered wild plants.

Among the many varieties of wild plants the Yakima women gathered for food was bitterroot. The woman in this 1911 photograph is drying bitterroot in the sun in preparation for storage.

At the beginning of August, the Yakima traveled southward and came together at the root-digging grounds in Klikitat territory. There they also traded with other Indian groups and fished for trout. In the middle of the month, huckleberries (*wíwnu*) ripened in the mountains. To celebrate, the Yakima held the year's final first-foods feast. Small parties of women and girls, each accompanied by a boy or older man who looked after the welfare of the group, traveled to the timberline to pick the huckleberries growing there. Once picked, the berries were placed on a smoldering log to dry and then stored in folded and sewn cedar bark containers.

The Yakima stored all kinds of foods in woven baskets. Basketmaking was a specialized skill for which Columbia Plateau women were famous. To hold roots, they made Wasco baskets, or "Sally bags"—soft, cylindrical bags made of *taxús* (Indian hemp) and often decorated with human or animal figures using bear grass or cornhusks. They also wove large, flat, flexible stor-

The Yakima traditionally carved the horns of mountain goats into bowls. This one is decorated with images of human skeletons, as seen in the detail.

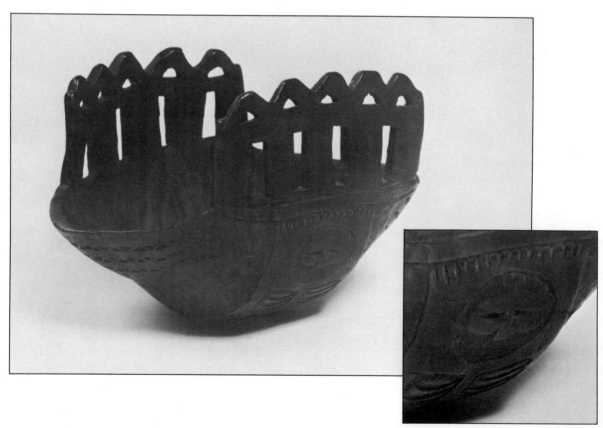

age wallets, known as cornhusk bags, or Nez Percé bags, although most Sahaptian women made them. Principally used for carrying and storing dried roots, they were twined from Indian hemp and decorated with an overlay of dyed corn husk, twine, or colored yarn.

Sahaptian basket makers were also known for their magnificent hard, coiled baskets that could hold a large quantity of roots, fruits, and berries. These were called Klikitat baskets, but they were made by other Plateau groups as well. Klikitat baskets were woven from cedar roots and decorated with overlapping designs of *yáy* (dyed ryegrass) from the mountains.

Some coiled baskets were used for cooking. These were woven so tightly that they could hold water without leaking and had tapered bottoms so that they could be wedged into the ground in an upright position. Water in these vessels could be brought to a boil quickly by dropping heated stones into the baskets.

In early autumn, families began to return to the river valleys for the fall fish runs. They also traveled to great trading centers on the Columbia. There the Yakima visited with friends and relatives from other villages and gathered up their stored food supplies. Some men went back to the mountains to hunt deer and elks.

In about mid-November, families returned to their village. They remained in these settlements throughout the winter and lived on the roots, berries, salmon, venison, and other foods they had preserved and stored in the previous months. The Yakima tended to establish their villages in clusters in river valleys, because these locations offered them protection from severe winter weather.

The average Yakima village had a population of between 50 and 200. However, a few very large settlements existed. The largest Yakima village, located near the present-day town of Union Gap, Washington, was regularly occupied by about 2,000 people. Several other large Yakima villages were located near the junction of the Yakima and Columbia rivers. The Walla Walla and Umatilla peoples also resided there.

The inhabitants of each permanent village recognized a certain portion of land around their settlement as their territory. However, they shared their hunting and gathering grounds with people in other villages, who in turn allowed others to use their lands. Fishing sites belonged to individuals or families, but, again, the owners readily gave other families permission to use these areas.

This spirit of reciprocity and generosity was seen in all dealings between local Yakima groups. The Yakima placed a high value on cooperation and hospitality, qualities that were well displayed at the yearly round of social activities in which all the groups participated. People looked forward each year to sponsoring or attending celebrations and renewing their friendships with inhabitants of other villages. These social ties contributed to the sense of unity the Yakima people already had because of their shared customs, language, interests, and beliefs.

One of the largest annual Yakima gatherings, or encampments, occurred in May and June at important digging grounds at two villages near what is now Kittitas, Washington. Alexander Ross, a fur trader who visited the Yakima in the early 19th century, described the encampment in June 1814 as "covering more than six miles in every direction." Ross also stated, "This mammoth camp could not have contained less than 3,000 men, exclusive of women and children, and treble that number of horses." Klikitat territory, home of close relatives living to the west, was also the scene of large gatherings, which featured extensive trading as well as horse races held on two famous tracks.

Another large summer encampment was held at the south end of Cle Elum Lake. There as many as 1,000 persons gathered in June and July to fish for salmon. At the beginning of August, people from various villages came together near present-day Teanaway, Washington, to gather the roots of camas plants in the meadows there. At both of these encampments, the Yakima visited, traded, played sports, and gambled. *Paalyút*, also known as the bone game or stick game, was a favorite activity and often lasted all night.

Women also played games with dice made from beaver teeth. Men competed in wrestling matches, foot races, shinny—a game similar to hockey—and other active sports. Klikitat territory was the location of other large gatherings. At these, Yakima and Klikitat traders met to conduct business.

At Celilo Falls and the Dalles, the Yakima traded with Indian peoples from the coast as well as with other Plateau groups. Popular exchange items included skins, furs, dried roots, berries, *ch?láy* (pulverized dried salmon), pemmican (a mixture of dried buffalo meat and animal fat), baskets, mats, basketry hats, mountain goat wool, buffalo and elk robes, horses, canoes, feathers, slaves, and weaving materials, such as bear grass, cedar and spruce roots, and wild hemp. Many of these goods were imported from the Great Plains of the central United States and from present-day northern California. Coastal Indians also brought some products unique to their homelands: eulachon (candlefish), dried seal meat, dried sturgeon, cured shellfish, whale blubber, and dogfish oil.

The standard currency was *haiqua*, the word in Chinook Jargon—the region's trade language—for dentalium. This shell was harvested from ocean beds off the west coast of present-day Vancouver Island. In addition to being the medium of exchange, dentalium was prized for making ornaments.

During the summer, the Yakima and people from coastal tribes gathered

Yakima women stored roots and fruits in baskets they wove from cedar roots or bark and decorated with ryegrass or bear grass.

in the mountains for regular trading ventures. The first intermarriages between these groups can be traced back to these mountain meetings. The Yakima also intermarried with other Plateau peoples, such as the Wenatchi, Wishham, Sk'ín, Klikitat, Walla Walla, Umatilla, Wyam, Wanapam, Nez Percé, and Palus. Through marriage ties, all these groups established a network of alliances that were further strengthened by their sharing of resources and settlement sites. These relationships produced a general climate of peaceful coexistence among the Yakima and their neighbors. Occasionally, hostilities would break out between various groups. But usually fighting would not involve large military forces.

Although the various local Yakima groups were united by a similar network of alliances, each village remained relatively independent—both free to make its own decisions and responsible for the actions of its own people. During the 1700s, however, there is evidence that a large portion of Yakima territory was united by a leader named We-ow-wicht. By means of conquest, he extended his influence from northern Yakima, or Kittitas, territory down the Yakima River to the sagebrush plains at the mouth of Toppenish Creek. We-ow-wicht died sometime before 1800. After his death, the unity of the various groups he conquered broke down. The territory was probably then divided among his eight sons, each inheriting a section over which he main-

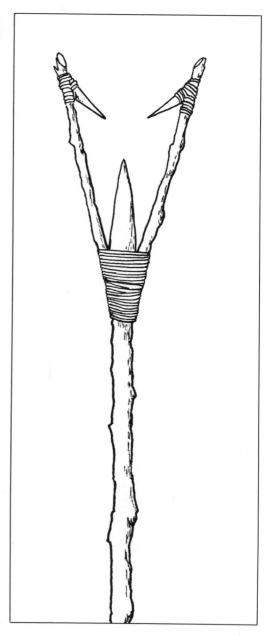

A leister, which was used by the Yakima to spear the many salmon and other fish found in local rivers.

tained limited control. Historical records confirm the existence of these brothers, as well as a sister whose son Kamiakin would become the Yakima's most influential leader in the mid-19th century. Many traditional Yakima individuals today trace their genealogies directly to this family.

Notwithstanding We-ow-wicht's short-lived confederacy, the small, independent village or band was traditionally the basic political unit of the Yakima, although rare formal alliances were made during wartime. Certain men were recognized as headmen or chiefs of their village. These positions tended to be inherited, and headmen were generally respected for their wisdom and generosity. Elderly women were also held in high regard and exerted influence over village decisions.

Several respected men of each village were chosen by consensus to be members of a council that helped the headman to settle disputes and maintain informal control over village activities and relations with other villages. The headman also had an assistant who went through the village every evening, repeating the headman's speeches in a loud voice and making announcements of important news. Another man, "the whipper," was charged with the responsibility of disciplining children who would not be quiet during ceremonies. Usually a family member's threat to summon the whipper was all that was needed to make a misbehaving youngster obedient.

Other leadership positions were held by men and women who were noted for their special skills as riders, hunters, fishers, root diggers, basketry weavers, ritual leaders, shamans (medicine doctors), orators, or warriors. Special status was also given to professional gamblers, outstanding athletes, people who owned many horses, and people who sponsored feasts and giveaways. Positions of leadership had a tendency to overlap. For instance, a headman might also be skilled at hunting and rich in horses.

Households of extended families were the basic social unit within Yakima villages. A village contained between 5 and 15 lodges, each of which housed several couples and their children who were all related by blood or marriage. Usually at least three generations—grandparents, parents, and children—lived together. People's other close relatives often lived in neighboring lodges.

The earliest Yakima lodges were pit houses. The builders of these dwellings began by digging a circular pit, 3 to 4 feet deep and 12 to 18 feet in diameter. Over the pit they then constructed a frame of light wooden poles, which they covered with mats and grass and banked on the outside with up to three feet of earth. A hole was left in the center of the roof, through which smoke from fires set within the lodge could escape. The hole also served as an entrance and exit and was reached by climbing a ladder made from a notched log. Alexander Ross described these homes as roomy, comfortable, and warm.

Over time, the size and shape of the Yakima's dwellings changed. By the early 18th century, they began to build four-walled, A-frame structures called *káatnams*. These probably became popular when the Yakima acquired horses because they could be easily dismantled and moved and therefore were an efficient adaptation to the mobile way of life the horse made possible. Each káatnam had a wooden frame that at its base measured from 40 to 60 feet long and 12 to 15 feet wide. Two of the walls leaned toward each other, meeting at the top of the dwelling, about 10 feet above the ground. The other two walls were rounded at the base. The pole framework was covered with several layers of stitched tule mats, and additional poles were then laid on top of the mats to hold them in place. The top of the dwelling was left open to release smoke from interior fires. Each family living in a lodge generally had its own fire. Doorways were made in the rounded ends of the dwelling, and a large section at the rear was reserved for racks on which the fish were hung to dry. Sometimes the outside walls were banked with earth to provide further protection from the wind and cold.

When traveling to fishing and gathering sites, families set up smaller, conical mat-covered lodges that could be easily carried on sleds called travois that were pulled by dogs or horses. On short hunting trips to the mountains, a mat lean-to or temporary shelter of brush was used. When the Yakima began to hunt for bison on the Plains, they adopted a skin-covered tipi typical of those used by Plains Indians.

Unlike many other American Indian societies, the Yakima regarded both their father's and mother's family members as blood relatives. (This system of determining kinship is the same used in American society today.) But families that were linked by marriage also felt special ties to one another. These ties were formally recognized by feasts and a series of ritual gift exchanges.

One of the most important of these was the wedding trade, which often took place after the birth of a couple's first child. The wife's family would invite the husband's family to a feast. There the hosts would offer their new in-laws *pshátani* goods—women's gifts such as baskets, decorated cornhusk bags filled with dried roots and berries, and strings of beads made of glass, shell, and bone all wrapped in a tule mat. Sometime later, the husband's family would host a feast and present their in-laws with *shaptákay* goods, men's gifts such as blankets and tanned hides, carried in a rawhide container known as a shaptákay. The wedding trade was the first formal public recognition of a marriage. Before it was held, however, a man and a woman lived together with one of the two families, usually the woman's. These unions were arranged by the families of the young man and woman, but only after the permission of the couple had

A Yakima tule mat lodge, photographed in 1911. These portable dwellings consisted of a wooden-pole frame covered with sewn mats.

been secured. Sometimes leaders who were wealthy enough to support more than one wife practiced polygyny.

Soon after a Yakima infant was born, it was placed on a baby carrier made of wood and buckskin called a cradleboard. (Babies were referred to as *skínpah*, meaning "person from the cradleboard place.") Cradleboards were often decorated with colored beads and other trinkets. A hoop made from a bough of a wild rosebush was placed over the infant's head to protect the baby against harm. A little buckskin bag containing the infant's umbilical cord was then hung from the hoop to ensure that the child would grow up healthy and have a long life.

Securely strapped into this protected buckskin home, a baby could easily be carried anywhere its family went. Yakima children spent most of their infancy in cradleboards. Whenever they outgrew one, a larger one was made. This continued until a child was weaned at about three years of age.

Probably the closest relationship between relatives sharing a lodge was that between children and their grandparents. While parents and young adults were away fishing, hunting, and gathering wild foods, grandparents looked after the children. It was grandparents who taught youngsters to respect the traditional Yakima way of life and showed them by example the proper way for a Yakima to behave. An unusual custom that grandchildren and grandparents had of addressing each other by the same kinship terms demonstrated the particularly important connection between them.

The importance of the individual from infancy on was stressed among the Yakima. A young person was taught to be self-sufficient and the

A Yakima infant secured in a cradleboard, photographed in the early 20th century.

rights of young children were respected. At the same time, children were also taught to respect the rights of others.

Children learned about the activities they would perform as adults by imitating their parents. Boys were taught to hunt, to fish, and to catch and break wild horses. Girls were given small baskets and encouraged to gather fruits and nuts. Their efforts were rewarded at special community feasts and giveaways. These were hosted by a child's family after he or she had performed an impressive feat. For instance, a family might host a feast after a boy shot his first deer or made his first significant catch of fish or after a girl gathered her first large basket of roots or berries. At ceremonies to celebrate other occasions—such as the first time a child danced in public—families would also give gifts to guests to thank them for giving recognition to their youngsters' accomplishment. The young people themselves did not receive presents; instead their reward was public recognition and praise. In this way, the Yakima honored and encouraged children's active participation in their society.

When a boy of about 13 began to do a man's work, he was called *winsh*, meaning "man." After a girl's first menses, she became a *tmáy*, or "a girl who is ready for marriage." At this time, she usually began an *itítamat*, or a "counting-the-days ball," which was similar to a diary. This ball was wound from a string of Indian hemp, on which a woman tied a knot or added a shell or bead to record every significant event of her life, such as her first courtship, her marriage, and the birth of her children. When a woman died, her counting-the-days ball was buried with her.

Adult men and women had different and separate responsibilities, but they also cooperated in performing many tasks. Men caught and broke horses; women packed them for travel. Men erected the pole scaffolding for longhouses and covered them with tule mat siding; women made the mats that covered the lodge and those used inside for bedding, partitions, floor coverings, and wrapping stored food. Men tied the three-pole foundation for Yakima tipis; women set them up and took them down. Men hunted, fished, and participated in raiding. Women gathered staple vegetable foods, preserved all types of foods, dressed skins and furs, and made decorated clothing, baskets, and other items that were given as gifts or used in the household. Men prepared meats for special occasions and to feed visitors. Women carried wood and water, and cooked.

All the food staples and household equipment that a woman processed were considered her property. Except for men with large herds of horses, women often accumulated more material wealth than men. Many of these articles became part of ceremonial exchanges or gift giving, conferring considerable prestige on the women who gave them.

When a person died, everyone related to the deceased by blood or through marriage drew together for mutual support. People often traveled long distances to attend a funeral. Some relatives brought food to help feed the crowd; others helped to prepare meals and serve those in attendance. Funeral services traditionally lasted five days and nights. Kinfolk and friends circled the body and sang, accompanied by drumbeats, to help send the spirit of the deceased to its final resting place. After the body was buried, a special mourning rite and a giveaway was held, and the dead person's lodge was burned down. As one Yakima elder explained: "It is a part of our heritage, to give away or destroy what the dead has touched and handled, where the dead has lived, so the family won't grieve when they see those things." If the deceased had been married, a ritual gift exchange between the couple's families took place, and the families' close ties continued. About a year after the funeral, a final memorial giveaway was held, at which the heirs distributed gifts in honor of the dead. The deceased's family was then released from mourning and once again could participate in ceremonies and other community events.

The Yakima's religion helped guide them not only during special ritual occasions but also throughout the activities of their everyday life. Some of their most ancient religious beliefs and practices concerned the powers of *tákh*— guardian spirits who protected people and gave them special abilities. Yakima individuals obtained guardian spirits as children by undertaking a vision quest.

During this ritual, a child was sent alone to a remote, isolated place, often in the mountains, where spirits were known to go. The child stayed in this spot for as briefly as overnight or for as long as several days, waiting for a vision of a spirit helper. If a spirit appeared, it would give the youngster special instructions about its power and how the child could use it. The spirit might also tell the boy or girl how to dress or paint his or her face and honor the power through song and dance. After returning from vision quests, children never discussed what they had seen and learned: People did not talk about spirit power.

If a child had obtained power from a guardian spirit, the youngster would begin to exhibit symptoms of "spirit sickness" at a later time. A *twáti*, or medicine doctor, would be called in to help the patient bring out the power he or she had received and understand how to use and express it properly.

If a Yakima had been gifted with guardian spirit power, he or she could participate in special winter spirit dances or medicine sings known as *wáanpsha*, meaning "power" or "spirit singing." These were held in lodges between December and mid-March. Wáanpsha was usually sponsored by the family of someone who had been troubled with spirit sickness and had been cured.

Wáanpsha lasted for five nights. (Five was the special "power number" of medicine sings.) People with guardian spirit power expressed it by singing and dancing. They were accompanied by a group of drummers, who pounded sticks or canes against a long plank resting on the ground. Other helpers also cooked and served food to the participants. The sponsors gave gifts to everyone who had helped with the winter spirit dance.

Spirit sickness was just one of many illnesses that the Yakima believed could be caused by supernatural agents or events. Sacred objects were believed to be inherently dangerous; only people with proper training were thought to be able to handle them without harm. People believed evil thoughts and harmful spirit power could also be used to bring others misfortune. Individuals who broke moral rules feared that supernatural beings would punish them with illness or accidents.

If a person became ill and supernatural powers were suspected to be the cause, a twáti was called to the home of the patient to bring about a cure. The medicine doctor would arrive wearing the special insignia of his profession: a bear claw necklace, a coyote or wolf headdress, and a rattle made of the dewclaws of a deer. The twáti then sang his power songs, accompanied by drummers. Sometimes he passed his hands over the patient's body, pressing and massaging certain areas to remove the source of the illness. For other ailments, he might cure the patient by sucking out the offending disease by using a special sucking tube. In some cases, the twáti gave the patient a native herbal medicine to drink.

The Yakima had an extensive knowledge of native plants that could be used to treat sores, infections, colds, burns, bruises, and even toothaches. Female medicine doctors in particular were skilled in using plants and herbs

Strings from several itítamat, *or counting-the-days balls, which Yakima women used like diaries. Each knot, bead, and shell tied onto a string represented a major event in the life of its owner.*

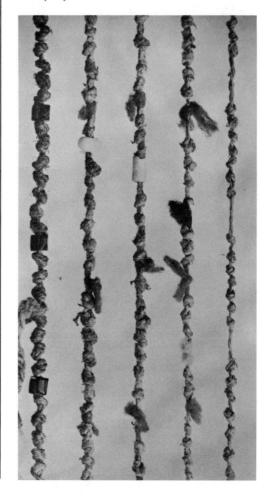

to make healing broths, emetics to induce vomiting, and poultices to stop bleeding.

In addition to curing, medicine doctors were called upon to bring changes in the weather, to foresee the future, to find lost objects, or to impart unusual power to an object. One story famous among the Yakima tells of a hunting rifle that had the power to shoot bullets that would kill whatever they hit without causing a wound.

The twáti had many skills because they had acquired the most powerful guardian spirit of all, T'amánws. This gave them the ability to control and overcome other spirit powers. As both physician and protector, the twáti were held in very high regard. But because the twáti could use their powers for harm as well as good, they were also feared.

Another powerful guardian spirit was Xwí-ach, the sweatlodge, which could restore its recipients' spiritual and physical purity as well as give him or her protection. Xwí-ach also cured disease, assured success in fishing and hunting, gave good fortune in gambling and courting, and removed the dangers associated with death. The best medicine doctors received their powers from Xwí-ach.

Sweatlodges were always built along running streams. They were small, dome-shaped structures made of a framework of arched willow branches that was covered with mats and earth. Inside, the ground was carpeted with fir or cedar boughs. Outside, a fire was

built, into which stones were placed. Once these were heated, they were raked into a shallow pit just inside the entrance of the sweatlodge. After the entrance was sealed shut, water was sprinkled onto the hot stones to form dense clouds of steam. People sat in the steam and sang various chants as they sweated from the heat. They then rushed out of the sweatlodge and dove into the cold stream nearby. This procedure was repeated several times. The bathers believed that this cleansed them not only of dirt but also, and more important, of illness, spiritual impurities, and other dangers to their well-being.

Shrines to guardian spirits were scattered throughout Yakima country and were especially common in the mountains. One popular shrine in the center of Yakima country was known as a "wishing place." There young and old alike came to ask for certain favors. Yakima legend explains the origin of this sacred place. Long ago, two giant women known as *tatatlíya* used to eat the animal people who inhabited the earth. The tatatlíya were caught by Speelyáy. He told them to stop because the people who were coming to live there soon would need the animals. The giant women then began a journey through the Yakima Valley to the Columbia River to search for other foods. Just before reaching Dry Creek, they collapsed from starvation and died. According to the Yakima, two barren areas, which they called *shapúkaniksh* ("to lay down flat on the back with limbs outstretched"), marked the spot where the giant women fell. At this site, the Yakima laid stones to form an outline of a large figure. A person seeking to make a wish would stand at the figure's head and throw a token toward a stone that represented its heart. People placed tokens underneath or around the other stones. Today a visitor might find scattered about the site bits of cloth, coins, part of a cradleboard, fragments of beadwork, or other symbols of petitions made in the past.

Many of the Yakima's other beliefs about spirits are explained in their legends. For instance, one story tells of ghosts who are attracted to people but who can be warded off by those car-rying a piece of a wild rosebush. Another explains that owls, as creatures of the night, can predict death or serious accidents. More humorous are the tales of "stick Indians"—small, mischievious imps who can imitate people and birds. Stick Indians were said to play pranks on people when they slept in the mountains. A Yakima woman recalled her father's advice for dealing with these nuisances:

> My dad used to tell us that they like matches. If you want to get rid of stick Indians, throw unlit matches at them. Throw them away from your camp, and they'll take them and go away, leave you alone.

A perforated deerskin shirt of a twáti, *or medicine doctor.* Twáti *used their special powers to cure patients struck with illnesses caused by supernatural beings.*

A second complex of traditional Yakima religious beliefs was known as Wáashat, the longhouse, seven drum, or Indian religion. Wáashat remained distinct from beliefs about guardian spirit powers and curing. There were no curing rituals in the longhouse religious service. As one Yakima elder has explained, "Wáashat is just pure faith. Just prayers."

The Northern Sahaptin word for "dance," Wáashat was popularly called the "Indian worship." Wáashat developed from an older religious movement known on the Columbia Plateau as the Prophet Dance, named after the many Indian prophets who, during the turbulent 18th and 19th centuries, received visions for bringing about a better world for their people. Wáashat contained many elements of the Yakima's ancient religious observances, such as the first-foods feast. The Yakima considered it to be their native religion, a perception that continues in the 20th century: The Yakima Nation's centennial bulletin, published in 1955, stated, "The old tribal religion was always followed since time immemorial. . . . It was called Wáashat."

Originally the services were held in the mat lodge of a headman. By the mid-19th century, the Yakima began to construct larger lodges, which they called longhouses. These were used exclusively for Wáashat services and as a community meeting place. Wáashat prayers were also sung before public tribal celebrations and commemorative and memorial services.

Inside the longhouses, the participants were separated by sex. Women, girls, and young children stood together along the longhouse's southern wall; men and boys, along its northern wall. All faced the center. People dressed in their finest ceremonial clothing and painted their face in honor of the occasion. Some of the worshipers held treasured feather fans in their right hand. Andrew J. Splawn, an early white settler in the Yakima Valley, described some of the rituals held in a 100-foot mat-covered longhouse at the Kittitas council and root-digging grounds in 1871. The Indians wore beaded buckskins with dentalia and wampum shell necklaces, and their faces were painted red and yellow.

Drummers sat or stood in a line, arranged by age and experience, along the western end of the longhouse facing the door. They used 3 to 7 sacred hand-painted, single-headed drums that were about 3 inches deep and 20 inches in diameter. Starting with the youngest, each drummer in turn began a song. To the right of this line, the ritual leader of the services stood, holding a brass bell, which was used as a "song counter" just as a conductor uses a baton. The participants danced and sang in time to the rhythm of the bell and drums.

During the Wáashat service, participants sang several series of seven songs. (Seven was the sacred number of Wáashat.) The worshipers stood and danced in place. At the end of a song, they raised their right hand in unison, saying, "á'y'y'" in a high tone that

A sweatlodge on Toppenish Creek on the Yakima Indian Reservation, photographed in the 1960s. Sweatlodge bathers sprinkled water on heated rocks just inside the entrance to fill the lodge with steam. After building up a sweat, the bathers dove into a nearby stream, a ritual that cleansed them physically and spiritually.

trailed off as they slowly lowered their arm and turned counterclockwise. This ending was said to be a benediction similar to "amen" in Christian church services. Turning in place was said "to release us from troubles." Sometimes a special children's dance was per-

formed, during which boys and girls moved to the right in a circle in the center of the floor with a fast, hopping step.

Between the series of seven songs, elders came forward to "speak out" to the children and young adults in a soft, low voice with their head bowed:

An early-20th-century photograph of a bell ringer and seven drummers—participants in a Wáashat, or Indian longhouse religious service—outside a longhouse in Wapato, Washington.

Remember the teachings of your grandparents. Be of one thought and heart, that's our belief. Keep an open home. Help one another. Be good to old people. The more you give, the more you receive; that's our Indian ways.

In this way, young people were reminded of the values that should guide their life.

A community dinner or ritual feast was a customary part of Wáashat ser-vices. Before the dinner, a bell was rung, a signal for everyone to stand and join in singing a prayer. The bell was rung again, and all intoned the word *chíish* (water) and sipped water from their cup. Then the feast began. Those present took a sip of water once again at the end of the meal just before a final prayer and tolling of the bell.

Water was an essential part of all longhouse rituals and had deep symbolic significance for the Yakima. One Yakima has said:

Water is the element which supplies all life, all plant and animal life. . . . In our religion water is our sacrament. I know that if we don't have water, there will be no life.

Like chíish, *tichám* (earth) had special meaning for the people. Traditionally, a longhouse had a smooth, hard-packed earthen floor on which the people danced in direct contact with the earth. Today this is no longer practical to maintain. Only one longhouse, located at Priest Rapids, has retained this sacred feature. However, tichám has kept its special significance. It is the subject of a moving prayer, which is loosely translated as, "Earth's body is everlasting. Earth's heart is everlasting. There is everlasting life and breath on earth."

For many thousands of years, the Yakima developed and maintained a unique way of life. As in all societies, their social and political systems ordered their world, and their religious beliefs gave meaning to their life. The balance of the Yakima world, however, would be disturbed when, in the 19th century, the people came into contact with a very different society—that of white Europeans and Americans. Although the world of these whites would be affected by their encounters with the Yakima, the Yakima's society would be radically transformed by the clash of two very different cultures. ▲

Two Yakima men on horseback in 1911. Horses represented the first non-Indian influence on the Yakima. Beginning in the 1700s, they acquired the animals from Shoshone traders who obtained them in the Southwest, where horses had been introduced centuries before by Spanish explorers.

A

CHANGING
SOCIETY

Before the 18th century, the Yakima were untouched by the influences of non-Indians. Their territory was one of the most isolated regions of the Columbia Plateau. To the west was the natural barrier of the Cascade Mountains. To the east was the buffer of other Plateau Indian groups.

But by 1730, dramatic changes had begun to take place in the Yakima homeland. At this time, bands of Shoshone Indians living to the south started to trade horses to the Nez Percé, the Cayuse, the Flathead, and other Plateau Indians, including the Yakima. The Shoshone acquired the animals from Indian groups in what is now the American Southwest, where horses had been introduced by Spanish explorers in the early 16th century.

Horses quickly became an important part of Yakima life. The rich natural grasslands of the mountain valleys and volcanic plains provided excellent grazing lands. Because of this environment and because Yakima country was fairly difficult for Indian horse raiders to reach, the size of the Yakima's herds increased rapidly. As early as 1811, the Yakima themselves had begun to sell and trade horses to other Plateau Indians. The animals eventually replaced dentalium as the basic medium of exchange in the Yakima's trade dealings.

The introduction of the horse brought about significant changes in both the Yakima's subsistence and social activities. On horseback, the Yakima could journey up to 70 miles a day, an impossible feat when traveling on foot using dog travois. This new mobility gave households and entire villages access to more extensive food resources, which enabled the Yakima to increase their food surpluses and economic security. Horses also made it possible to travel easily to intertribal trade centers and social gatherings. Horse racing competitions between villages and tribes were popular at these events. Skill in handling and racing horses became a source of prestige.

Horses also allowed the Yakima to cross the Rocky Mountains and move eastward onto the Great Plains. Following the example of the Indian tribes native to the Plains, they learned to hunt the buffalo that roamed in large herds throughout the region. Although the Yakima greatly desired buffalo meat and hides, they remained essentially a fishing and gathering people.

The Yakima's contact with Plains tribes increased during the 18th and 19th centuries, but none of these groups' cultural institutions made their way into Yakima country. However, the trade goods the Yakima obtained from Plains Indians had a substantial influence on their way of life. The Yakima abandoned their traditional clothing made from sagebrush, shredded cedar, and willow bark in favor of buckskin clothing in the style worn by the Crow, Blackfeet, and Sioux Indians. Men dressed in breechcloths, leggings, and shirts. Women's dresses were made from two buckskins that were laced or sewn together at the shoulders and the sides. Both sexes wore strings of beads and high, soft-soled moccasins. The Yakima's buckskin clothing was often decorated with beads, porcupine quills, fringes, and elk teeth.

War bonnets made of eagle feathers were also introduced by Plains groups. These became a symbol of prestige among the Yakima. Head roaches, hairbone breastplates, and feather bustles also became popular attire for dances and other celebrations.

The Yakima replaced their portable, conical mat-covered lodges with skin-covered tipis like those used by Plains Indians. They also adopted Plains-style rawhide pack bags, known as parfleches, which they used in addition to their traditional baskets as carrying and storage cases. Other Plains influences were catlinite pipes, buffalo horn headdresses, tanned and decorated buffalo robes, and extensively beaded horse trappings made for favorite mounts.

Among the items the Yakima and other Plateau Indians received through trade at this time were European and American goods. Non-Indian traders first introduced these goods to the Indians on the Plains and on the Pacific Coast. Gradually, through trade between tribes, the objects filtered inland into Yakima territory from the east and west. By the end of the 18th century, metal knives, hatchets, copper cooking kettles, brass bells, blue and white glass beads, and metal bracelets were available at the great trading centers at the Dalles.

At this time, the Yakima were exposed to another non-Indian influ-

After the acquisition of horses gave the Yakima increased mobility, they began to use portable deerskin tipis like those of Indian tribes on the Great Plains.

ence—one that was to have tragic consequences. Along with trade goods, whites unknowingly gave the Indians they encountered European diseases, such as smallpox and measles. These diseases were not endemic in North America, so Indians had developed no immunities to them and usually died quickly after exposure to people carrying the germs. Deadly epidemics began to spread along the Columbia River, the Indians' main artery of travel. The earliest smallpox epidemic swept across the continent from the Missouri River area to the Pacific Coast in about 1775; the disease was probably spread by infected Plateau buffalo hunters who returned to the region from the Plains. The impact on tribes along the middle Columbia River was considerable.

About 30 years later, the Yakima had their first direct contact with non-

This mural in Oregon's state capitol rotunda depicts explorers Meriwether Lewis and William Clark at Celilo Falls on the Columbia River in 1805. The members of the Lewis and Clark expedition were the first non-Indians to have direct contact with the Yakima.

Indians. At the request of President Thomas Jefferson, explorers Meriwether Lewis and William Clark led an expedition in 1803–6 that sought to chart an overland route from the eastern portion of the United States to the Pacific Ocean. In 1805, Lewis and Clark had followed the course of the Snake River to its junction with the Columbia. From there, they traveled a few miles upstream to the mouth of Yakima River.

After reports of Lewis and Clark's expedition were made public, American and Canadian fur trappers and traders soon rushed to the Pacific Northwest. Increasingly, they began to travel up the Columbia River as they competed for control of the Plateau's resources. The first fur trading post on the Columbia, Fort Astoria, was established at the river's mouth in 1811 by American employees of the Pacific Fur Company. The post was sold to the British-owned North West Company in 1813 and renamed Fort George. The journals of the fur traders at these posts contain descriptions of the various Indian peoples they met, including the Yakima. For instance, Alexander Ross, who traveled up the Columbia River in 1811 and visited a Yakima encampment in the Kittitas Valley in 1814, wrote the following about the people:

> The men were generally tall, raw-boned, and well dressed; having all buffalo robes, deer-skin leggings, very white and most of them garnished with porcupine quills. Their shoes were also trimmed and painted red. . . . Altogether their appearance indicated wealth. . . . The women wore garments of well dressed deer-skin down to their heels; many of them richly garnished with beads, higuas [dentalium], and other trinkets—leggings and shoes similar to those of the men. Their faces were painted red. . . . [Some] were armed with guns, and the others with bows and arrows. . . . The plains were literally covered with horses, of which there could not have been less than four thousand in sight of the camp.

Most of the early fur traders described the Indians in this part of the Plateau as affluent, helpful, and friendly.

Aside from sporadic meetings, the Yakima initially had relatively little contact with white fur traders. However, their interaction increased after 1825, when the Hudson's Bay Company, which had merged with the North West Company, established a trading post named Fort Vancouver 85 miles upriver from Fort George. Fort Vancouver rap-idly became a popular center for British traders. The Yakima began to make trips to the post and to others later built by the Hudson's Bay Company. These included Fort Walla Walla, located near the confluence of the Snake and Columbia rivers, and Nisqually House, which was to the west of the Cascade Mountains near the head of Puget Sound. The British trade goods the Indians wanted most were guns and ammunition for hunting. Other items they sought were tobacco, blankets, beads, and metal goods—such as axes, knives, and projectile points. The Yakima had enough surplus horses to trade for most of the objects they wanted, and relations between the Indians and the Hudson's Bay Company remained good. However, the company did not encourage any whites to settle in the Plateau country, except those involved in trading.

The Yakima were experiencing other economic changes in the early 19th century. Hudson's Bay Company employees had brought several thousand longhorn cattle to the region from present-day California and the herd was improved with cows obtained from white settlers. In about 1840, a Yakima leader named Kamiakin traded some of his horses for cattle at Fort Vancouver and established the first cattle herd in the Yakima Valley. The longhorns thrived on the rich bunchgrass in the hill country. A short time later, another Yakima leader, Owhi, obtained some cattle at Fort Nisqually and drove them over the Cascades and down into Yakima country. Other Indians soon followed their example, and beef became a staple of the Yakima diet.

At this time, the Indians also began to cultivate gardens, using seeds and plants they obtained from the Hudson's Bay Company. By the mid-19th century, the Yakima were raising potatoes, melons, squash, barley, and Indian corn. They usually dug their gardens near streams so that they could water them easily. Kamiakin even dug irrigation ditches to his gardens.

Through their contact with whites, the Yakima became familiar with many imported goods and technological conveniences, particularly utensils and firearms. As their knowledge of non-Indian ways increased, some began to seek wage work as boatmen, porters, and house servants in the nearby towns of Vancouver and Portland. However, the Yakima were not dependent on non-Indians or manufactured goods. For instance, the Indians continued to make their own baskets, fishing equipment, and saddles.

After 1835, white settlers began to flock westward along a route between Independence, Missouri, and Fort Vancouver known as the Oregon Trail. Their destination was the rich lands of the Willamette Valley near present-day Portland, Oregon. Because Yakima territory was not prime farming country, the Yakima were at first relatively undisturbed by these newcomers.

In the 1840s, the Yakima encountered another American expedition sent to study their lands. These explorers, led by Lieutenant Charles Wilkes, were sent by the U.S. government to travel from the Pacific Coast eastward over the Cascades into Yakima territory. The party recorded meeting several Yakima chiefs and witnessing some curing rituals and first-foods ceremonies.

Soon after the Wilkes expedition, Yakima territory became part of the United States. For decades, the United States and England had both claimed that they owned Oregon Country, a vast area along the west coasts of present-day Canada and the United States. In 1846, the two countries settled the dispute by agreeing to split the territory along the 49th Parallel. The United States thereby obtained land south of this boundary, including what are now Washington, Oregon, northern Idaho, and western Montana. In 1848, the United States formally organized this area as Oregon Territory, and Hudson's Bay Company moved its headquarters from Fort Vancouver to Vancouver Island in British Columbia, Canada.

In the 1830s and 1840s, the Yakima came under another non-Indian influence—missionaries who sought to convert them to Christianity. A group of Methodist ministers crossed the continent with an expedition led by Nathaniel Wyeth and settled at Fort Vancouver in 1834. They later moved south to the Willamette Valley. In 1838, others founded a mission at the Dalles. Two years earlier, two Catholic priests of the Oblate order had begun missionary work in the middle Columbia River area. These missionaries were followed by Marcus Whitman, a Presbyterian minister who settled near a Hudson's Bay Company trading post to the southeast of Yakima country in the territory of the Cayuse Indians in 1838.

To compete with the Protestant missions to the south and east of Yakima lands, Oblate fathers Raschal Richard and E. C. Chirouse established St. Rose, the first Christian mission among the Yakima, at Toppenish Creek in 1847. Two years later, they were joined by three more priests, including Father Jean Marie Charles Pandosy, and built a second mission, St. Joseph, near Kamiakin's home along the Ahtanum Ridge. The impact of these missionaries on the Yakima's spiritual life was minimal at this time. Most Yakima, including Kamiakin, refused to be baptized because the priests wanted them to stop the practice of polygyny. But men did not want to give up their wives or the high prestige that polygynists had in Yakima society. Despite this disagreement, the priests and the Yakima were friendly. The Oblate fathers even helped teach the Indians how to improve their gardening and irrigation techniques. Father Pandosy also began a study of the Yakima language and published the first grammar and dictionary in 1862.

An engraving of Fort Vancouver, which the Hudson's Bay Company established as the headquarters for its fur trading operations in 1825. At this trading post, the Yakima obtained guns, ammunition, blankets, beads, seeds, and cattle from white traders.

The Whitman mission in 1843. The mission was established by Presbyterian minister Marcus Whitman in Cayuse Indian country to the southeast of Yakima territory.

A less harmonious relationship developed between the Cayuse and the Presbyterians at the Whitman mission. In 1847, a measles epidemic brought by non-Indians traveling along the Oregon Trail spread through the Columbia Plateau. Indians died in vast numbers. The Cayuse accused Whitman's missionaries of causing the illness and killed 14 of them. In retaliation, a group of non-Indian volunteers in the Oregon territorial militia pursued the murderers. This conflict erupted into the Cayuse War of 1848, which marked the beginning of hostilities between white settlers and Plateau Indians. Un-

fortunately, additional confrontations would follow.

The Yakima's relations with Americans began to worsen after 1850, when the U.S. Congress passed the Donation Act. This legislation permitted white homesteaders to settle on Indian lands along the northwest coast. The number of whites from the East migrating to the lands west of the Cascade Mountains soon increased dramatically.

This influx was in part to blame for the severe smallpox epidemic that broke out in Yakima territory in 1852–53. Two out of every five Yakima died. George Gibbs, a government employee, reported that "the whole course of the Yakima [River] is lined with the vestiges of former villages now vacant." Between 1805 and 1853, the Yakima population declined from about 7,000 to 2,000. Clearly, epidemics took a devastating toll on the people during their first years of contact with whites.

The non-Indian settlers in Oregon Territory soon began to pressure the U.S. government to partition the area. On March 3, 1853, the territory was divided into two parts, and the following May, portions of present-day Washington, Idaho, and Montana officially became Washington Territory. In that same year, the first large wagon train—composed of 155 people, led by John Longmire, and 36 wagons—passed through the Yakima Valley as a shortcut to the Puget Sound region. At this time, trading licenses that permitted settle-ment in Indian territory were also issued to suppliers for wagon trains.

Isaac I. Stevens, a 35-year-old West Point graduate and former army major, was appointed governor and superintendent of Indian affairs for the newly formed Washington Territory. These two responsibilities naturally represented a conflict of interests: As governor, Stevens was to serve the American settlers in the territory, but as superintendent of Indian affairs, he was charged with ensuring the well-being of the Indians native to the region. When Stevens arrived in Olympia, the territorial capital, on November 23, 1853, the white population of Washington Territory was only 3,965. The extraordinary rise in this number over the next decade would bear witness to which of Stevens's responsibilities he took more seriously. ▲

Yakima leader Kamiakin, drawn by Gustav Sohon, a U.S. military artist present at the treaty negotiations at Walla Walla in 1855.

THE TREATY ERA
AND
THE YAKIMA WARS

In the 1850s, Yakima leaders tried to unify their independent village groups for the first time since We-ow-wicht's short-lived confederacy dissolved in the 18th century. Political power and influence had become concentrated in the hands of a few influential headmen, several of whom were direct descendants of We-ow-wicht. They established two divisions in Yakima territory, with Wenas Creek as the boundary dividing them. To the south of the creek lived the Lower Yakima, who were led by three principal headmen—Kamiakin and his brothers Skloom and Showaway. To the north were the Upper Yakima, or Kittitas. Their leaders were Teias and Owhi, the uncles of the Lower Yakima headmen.

The move toward unification was a response to increasing threats posed by the white settlers who were encroaching upon Yakima lands and by officials of the federal government who wanted to take control of their territory. The influence of the government first began to be felt early in 1854, when the Columbia River Southern District Agency was established at Vancouver. This was a local office of the Bureau of Indian Affairs (BIA), the federal agency formed in 1824 to oversee all dealings between Indians and the U.S. government. The Vancouver agency was to have jurisdiction over all Indians living in Washington Territory. Soon a subagency was founded at White Salmon near the Dalles. Stationed there was Agent Andrew J. Bolon, the government's representive appointed to conduct all official business with the Yakima.

During the summer of 1854, a military party led by Captain George B. McClellan was dispatched to Yakima country. The men under McClellan's

Washington territorial governor and superintendent of Indian affairs Isaac I. Stevens.

command were to conduct a survey in preparation for the construction of a wagon road and railroad through the Indians' homeland. Governor Isaac Stevens told Agent George Gibbs to accompany McClellan's men. Stevens publicly said that Gibbs's duties were to explain the party's mission and secure the Yakima's permission and assistance in building the road.

In reality, Stevens wanted Gibbs to determine whether the Indians could be persuaded to cede their land to the U.S. government. The governor wanted the government to acquire title to Indian lands in Washington Territory so it could legally be opened for white settlement. He also hoped to relocate, or remove, the Indians to specific areas designated as reservations, to which they would have exclusive rights. Although this policy was presented as beneficial to Indians, reservations in fact were like concentration camps. They segregated Indians from the general populace, hindered their access to food resources, and confined them so that they could be more easily manipulated by the government.

McClellan's party met with Kamiakin at the Ahtanum mission near his home and with Owhi at his main camp on Wenas Creek. In Gibbs's report to Stevens on these meetings, the agent expressed great sympathy for the Yakima. He noted that the Yakima were friendly toward whites but concluded that this was true only because they had thus far had limited contact with white settlers and the U.S. government. In his

Gustav Sohon's drawing of Governor Stevens addressing the Indians he assembled at the Walla Walla Council, 1855.

report, Gibbs explicitly advised Stevens not to seek land cessions or attempt to place the Plateau Indians on reservations:

> It is not believed that extensive reserves would be desirable for these tribes. . . . They are not generally hunters; nor is their country any longer a game country. They require the liberty of motion for the purpose of seeking, in their proper season, roots, berries, and fish, where those articles can be found, and of grazing their horses and cattle at large. . . . In like manner, the use of their customary fisheries, and free pasturage for their stock on unenclosed lands, should be secured.

McClellan's report was in agreement. Stevens rejected McClellan's and Gibbs's recommendations and instead began to pressure the Indians of Washington Territory to agree to land cessions. During 1854, he negotiated a series of treaties with coastal Indians through which he obtained title to their lands. In the spring of 1855, he turned his attention to the Indians living to the east of the Cascades.

When it became clear that Stevens was bent on acquiring territory on the Plateau, Kamiakin called representatives of every major Salish and Sahaptian tribal group in the middle Columbia Plateau to a council in the Grand Ronde Valley in eastern Oregon. The purpose of the council was to form an intertribal confederacy for the groups' mutual protection and to organize their resistance against white occupancy of their lands. All the council representatives except for Lawyer of the Nez Percé and Garry of the Spokane opposed negotiating land cession treaties.

In spite of growing Indian unrest, Stevens continued to press for Indian treaties, land cessions, and removal to reservations. He sent James Doty, secretary of his treaty commission, to notify the interior Plateau Indians that they were to convene for a grand council at the end of May 1855. Representatives of these tribes were told to come to Camp Stevens in the Walla Walla Valley on Mill Creek at the location of the present-day city of Walla Walla. In ancient times, Indians had held council meetings at this site. At first, Kamiakin refused to come to the Walla Walla Council, but in the end he attended, having been designated as the principal Yakima chief.

Many large contingents of Indians—ranging in size from 300 Cayuse to 2,500 Nez Percé—arrived at Camp Stevens between May 24 and 28. Led by Kamiakin, Owhi, and Skloom, about 1,000 Yakima reached the council grounds on May 28. They were accompanied by groups of Walla Walla, Wenatchi, Palus, and Columbia River bands. Umatilla, Columbia-Sinkiuse, and members of other Plateau tribes also swarmed into the area. Governor Stevens arrived with Governor Joel Palmer of Oregon Territory and 40 armed troops. Several interpreters and other witnesses, including the Oblate priests E. C. Chirouse and Jean Marie Charles Pandosy, were also present. Colonel Lawrence Kip was designated to keep

a journal of daily activities.

Except for the presence of U.S. forces, the council resembled a typical Plateau intertribal gathering. Between 5,000 and 6,000 Indians were scattered in camps throughout the Walla Walla Valley. While there, they participated in horse races, stick and bone gambling games, singing, drumming, and dancing.

The Walla Walla Council officially convened on May 29 and continued until June 11. The discussions were lengthy, reflecting the confusion and resentment of the Indians present. According to Kip's record, tribal alliances and attitudes continually shifted during the negotiations. But one thing remained constant: With the exception of Lawyer, the Indian leaders continued to oppose the treaty provisions that Stevens presented them.

Much of the confusion at the council was due to Stevens's failure to understand that local bands of Plateau Indians were traditionally autonomous. He designated headmen of individual bands as "chiefs" and gave them authority over entire tribes. Sometimes, headmen's authority was extended to bands that were not represented at the treaty council but would be affected by the outcome of the negotiations. This was the situation for some independent Columbia River bands who were designated as Yakima. Although Stevens designated Kamiakin as the head chief of all the Yakima, the Indian leader never claimed that he had the right to

(continued on page 65)

FROM BARK TO BUCKSKIN

Traditionally the Yakima dressed in clothes woven from fibers of sagebrush and cedar bark. But about 1730, when bands of Shoshone Indians entered the Columbia Plateau from the south and began trading horses to the Yakima, this began to change. These horses—descendants of those brought to North America by Spanish explorers in the 16th century—enabled the Yakima to travel far afield to trade and brought them in contact with the buffalo-hunting tribes living to the east on the Great Plains. The Yakima adopted many aspects of Plains Indian culture, particularly the use of leather made from deer hides to make clothing, such as moccasins, and to build tipis for shelter.

The Yakima's new mobility also helped them acquire European glass beads, both from the Plains tribes and from tribes of the Pacific Coast to the west. Whites explored these areas—and traded beads and other goods to the tribes there—decades before they traveled inland as far as the Columbia Plateau, where the Yakima lived.

The beautiful Yakima garments shown on these pages illustrate how the settlement of Europeans on the fringes of North America affected a tribe deep in the interior long before that tribe came into contact with whites. They also hint at the vibrancy of intertribal trade and the shrewd flexibility of the Yakima people.

This beaded leather belt illustrates the Yakima's way of borrowing from other cultures to enrich their own. The Yakima first acquired leather-craft skills and European glass beads from other tribes. But the flower-and-leaf design used here suggests the tribe's affectionate relationship with the plant life of its own Columbia Plateau homeland.

From the Great Plains tribes, the Yakima learned to make leather moccasins
like these.

These buckskin gauntlets are decorated with a beaded floral design and with
fringe at the flared cuffs.

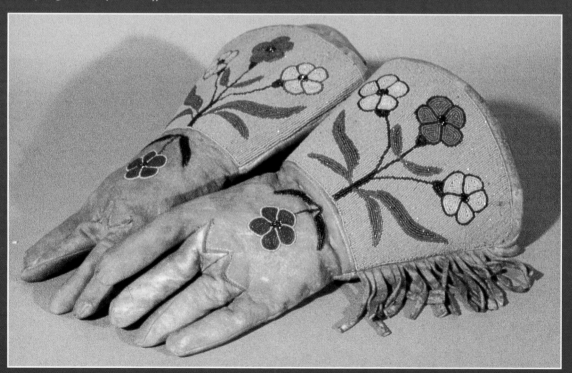

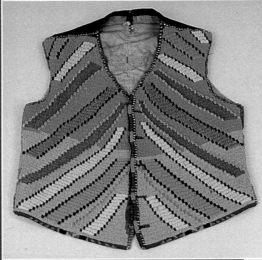

The imperfection in the bead design of the leather vest above attests to its handmade uniqueness. The yellow bar in the upper right corner has no mate on the left. In the vest at right, butterflies poise on flowers on both sides of the center opening.

This Yakima elk-skin dress bears a strong
resemblance to those worn by Plains women.

The cut of this wool dress is simple, but the dress
is richly adorned with beads and metal ornaments.

A man's elk-skin coat with fur trim and long fringe at the sleeves and shoulders.

Leather leggings were worn by Yakima horsemen to protect their legs from plants, such as sagebrush, a rough shrub common to arid regions.

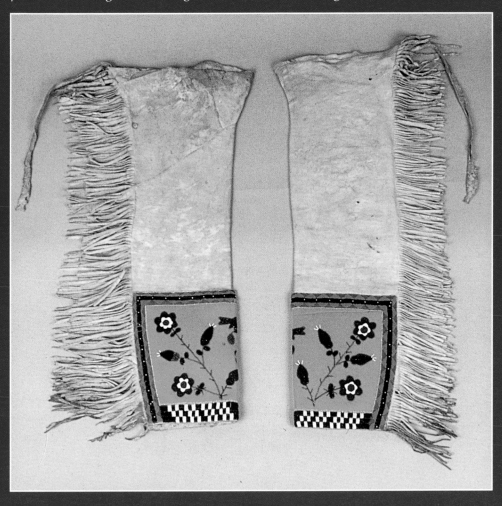

Though the Yakima were not known for their metalwork, these bracelets show skillful use of subtle, etched detail.

A necklace made from bear claws and beads.

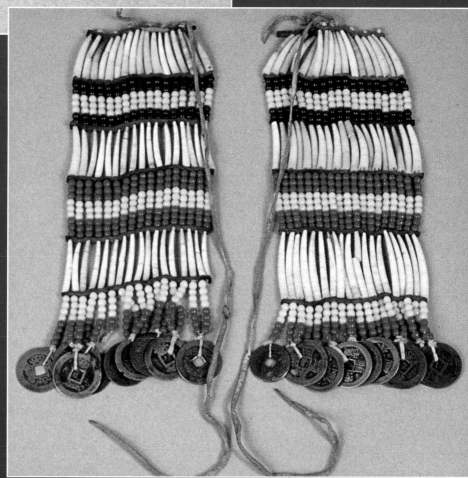

Head ornaments, like these made of beads and coins, were worn by Yakima brides.

This feathered headdress is a striking example of the Yakima's adoption of aspects of Plains Indian culture. Materials used include eagle feathers, horse-hair, canvas, ribbon, and glass beads of seven different colors.

(continued from page 56)

speak for all of these people. The governor also planned to place some separate, independent tribal groups on the same reservation, whether or not it was agreeable to them.

After several days of being pressured and threatened by the U.S. officials, Kamiakin and Peupeumoxmox, the Walla Walla chief, asked for a recess in the negotiations so that they would have more time to study the treaty provisions. Looking Glass, an important Nez Percé leader who had been hunting in buffalo country, then arrived belatedly on the scene. He immediately began to argue that the Indians should not sign the treaty. A dispute between various factions of Nez Percé followed. In the confusion, Stevens confirmed Lawyer as the head chief of the Nez Percé. In a private meeting with the governor, Lawyer agreed to sign a treaty on behalf of the Nez Percé. Stevens then offered to establish one reservation for just the Cayuse, Umatilla, and Walla Walla, and representatives from these tribes accepted his terms.

Yakima chiefs Kamiakin, Owhi, and Skloom still continued to oppose land cessions, but on June 9, 1855, they signed Stevens's treaty with an X. Kamiakin said he was tired of talking and wanted to get back to his garden. He explained that he had not wanted to be head chief, but his people had asked him to speak for them. The leader refused to accept from the U.S. officials any of the goods due to him according to the terms of the treaty. He said he would prefer to wait to receive them after the treaty was ratified by Congress and thus became official. (This would not take place until four years later in 1859.)

It is uncertain whether the Yakima chiefs understood that they were indicating their agreement to the treaty's terms by putting their mark on the document. Some Yakima witnesses later claimed that Kamiakin and Owhi "touched a stick while a little mark was made to show friendship only." James Doty's records pose other unresolved questions. In his private journal, he wrote that the signing took place on the evening of June 9th after the day's negotiations had been adjourned. Doty provides no details about the event in his official record.

The treaties negotiated at the Walla Walla Council provided for the creation of three reservations on the Columbia Plateau—one for the Nez Percé; one for the Walla Walla, Umatilla, and Cayuse; and one for the Yakima, which was to be located on the lands of the Lower Yakima.

The Yakima's 1855 treaty marked the beginning of the group's formal relationship with the U.S. government. Of equal significance, it also created a new political and social entity: the Consolidated Tribes and Bands of the Yakima Indian Nation.

The new Yakima Nation was to comprise 14 formerly independent bands or tribes, which thereafter would be treated as though they were a single tribe. These bands included the Yakima (spelled "Yakama" in the treaty), the

Palus ("Palouse"), the Wenatchi ("Pis-quouse"), the Wenatshapam fishery people in Wenatchi territory, the Kli-kitat, the Wishham at the Dalles, the Sk'in-pah, the Kah-milt-pah (a Rock Creek band of Yakima), and six other small bands of people who lived at various locations along the Columbia River from the Cascades upstream to Wen-atchi territory. All these people had long maintained close ties and alliances through marriage, the sharing of food and settlement sites, trade, and participation in intertribal gatherings. The Wanapam of Priest Rapids and several other bands with close connections to the Yakima were not named in the document, however.

Treaty signatories included 14 chiefs or headmen: Kamiakin, who was designated head chief of the new Yakima Nation; Owhi, the principal Upper Yakima headman; Skloom, representing the Lower Yakima bands; Me-ni-nock and 1 other Sk'in-pah headman; Elit Parker and another leader from Celilo; 3 Wishham headmen; another Yakima; a Palus; a headman from the Rock Creek band; and 1 unidentified person. The Wenatchi, Klikitat, and the six small Columbia River bands, which had been named as part of the Yakima Nation, were evidently not directly represented.

According to the treaty's terms, the people of the Yakima Nation ceded 10,800,000 acres (29,000 square miles) of land—more than one-fourth of the present-day state of Washington—to the U.S. government. Stevens had er-

roneously included in this area some territory that was occupied by Indian groups not named in the treaty, including the Columbia-Sinkiuse, Wanapam, Wauyukma, Umatilla, and Wayampam.

In return for relinquishing these lands, the people of the Yakima Nation retained a tract of about 1,200,000 acres (2,000 square miles) for their "exclusive use and benefit," to be held in trust by the U.S. government as an Indian reservation. (The area was first known as the Simcoe Reservation but later was renamed the Yakima Reservation.) The treaty stated that "[no] white man, excepting those in the employment of the [Bureau of Indian Affairs, shall] be permitted to reside upon the said reservation *without permission of the tribe* and the superintendent and agent." Furthermore, the Indians agreed to "remove to and settle upon the reservation within one year *after the ratification* of this treaty."

Other compensations were also guaranteed in the treaty. The United States was to pay the Yakima Nation $200,000, about 2.1 cents for every acre of land they ceded. In addition, it was to give them $140,000 in annuities (yearly payments) spread over a 20-year period and $60,000 to finance Indian families' removal to the reservation and to help them build fences around their farms, construct homes and other necessary buildings, and supply provisions and "outfits."

The government also promised to establish two schools on the reservation, one of which was to be an agricultural-industrial school, staffed with a superintendent and two teachers, that Indian children could attend without cost. Other facilities to be built were two blacksmith's shops, a gunsmith's shop, a carpenter's shop, a wagonmaker and plowwright's shop, a sawmill, and a flour mill. The United States would employ people to teach the Indians these trades. It would also provide the Yak-ima Nation with a doctor and a hospital. And with the nefarious practices of the traders in mind, alcohol was forbidden on the reservation.

To ensure the Yakima's access to the Wenatshapam fishery, the treaty stipulated that this area was "reserved and set apart for the use and benefit of the tribes and bands." Other treaty provisions guaranteed the Indians the right

An 1877 photograph of Nez Percé chief Looking Glass. The leader strongly opposed signing Governor Stevens's treaties.

Drawings by Gustav Sohon of Skloom and Owhi, two of the Yakima chiefs who signed the 1855 treaty with the U.S. government.

to fish in all their "usual and accustomed places," and to hunt, gather roots and berries, and pasture their horses and cattle on any open, unclaimed lands.

After the Walla Walla Council was concluded, Governor Stevens and a small party traveled eastward across the Rocky Mountains to Fort Benton. There they negotiated treaties with the Blackfeet and other tribes in the eastern portion of Washington Territory.

Within a month, Stevens placed advertisements in the *Puget Sound Courier* and two other territorial newspapers, announcing that the ceded lands on the Plateau were open to settlement by whites. The land rush was on. A flood of non-Indians trespassed over Indian lands, even over farms still worked by Indians. The settlers boldly grazed their cattle and sheep and cultivated crops

on lands to which they had no rights or title. Stevens's treaties had yet to be ratified by Congress, and until they were this area was still Indian territory.

The Indians' resentment of the intruders increased after gold was discovered in the vicinity of Fort Colville in northeastern Washington. To reach the new goldfields, prospectors from the Pacific Coast began crossing Yakima territory in direct violation of treaty terms. Tensions rose and open hostilities erupted when a group of Yakima men intercepted and killed some trespassing miners who had been molesting Yakima women.

On September 20, 1855, Agent Bolon, who had enjoyed friendly relations with the Yakima, left the subagency at the Dalles to investigate the killings. Bolon met Showaway at his home on Toppenish Creek. The leader advised him to turn back and leave Yakima country because the Indians were angry at all whites. He started to return to the Dalles, but along the way he was apprehended by a band of Indians and killed. Among this group was Showaway's son Mosheel.

When news of the murder reached the territorial authorities, Major Granville O. Haller was dispatched from Fort Dalles on October 2 with 102 troops and a cannon to avenge Bolon's death and suppress other Indian uprisings. Lieutenant W. A. Slaughter and a company of men were sent from the coast to support Haller. At Toppenish Creek, the major and his soldiers were attacked and routed by 700 Indians led by Kamiakin. Owhi's son, Qualchan, emerged as one of the group's leading warriors. Hearing of Haller's defeat, Slaughter's company fled. What had begun as a skirmish had erupted into a full-scale war.

Several tribes joined the Yakima in trying to drive the whites out of their country. The Columbia-Sinkiuse led by Chief Moses banded with Kamiakin, Owhi, and Qualchan. The Walla Walla under Chief Peupeumoxmox formed an alliance with the Palus, Umatilla, and Cayuse.

Major Gabriel J. Rains was sent into Yakima country to avenge Haller's defeat. Serving under his command was a West Point graduate named Philip Sheridan, who would later become famous as a general in the Civil War. The Oregon Mounted Volunteers, commanded by Colonel James W. Nesmith,

joined Rains in the field. In November 1855, the soldiers and volunteers advanced in force, pursuing the Indians to Union Gap, a town near the junction of Ahtanum Creek and the Yakima River. The Indians escaped across the river, taunting the military as they fled. The army then looted and burned the Catholic mission at Ahtanum, claiming that the Oblate fathers had been supplying the Indians with ammunition.

At the mission, Kamiakin had left a letter, which he dictated to Father Pandosy, that offered to end the hostilities. Rains's reply reflected his arrogance, anger, and frustration. It contained nothing but boastful threats that he would bring about the complete end and oblivion of the Yakima people.

In spite of his humiliating defeat, Haller spoke in defense of the Indians, stating that their actions were justified. He was highly critical of Rains's aggressive pursuit of the "hostiles," as was Lieutenant Sheridan in his account of the skirmish at Union Gap. Both Haller and Sheridan also maintained that the Oblates had been innocent of collaborating with the warriors and that the destruction of the mission had been unwarranted.

The territorial volunteers next rode into the Walla Walla Valley to the southeast. They pillaged the countryside for supplies and food, which they stole from French-Canadian farmers as well as from friendly Indians. When the volunteers reached Fort Walla Walla, the Indian alliance suffered its first crushing blow. Peupeumoxmox, who came to talk peace under a flag of truce, was taken into custody by Nesmith's men and brutally murdered. Parts of his mutilated body were taken by the volunteers for souvenirs. The Indians then scattered for the winter and warfare temporarily ceased.

Aware of the injustices and treaty violations that had provoked the Indians into war, several other members of the regular army came to their defense. General John E. Wool, commander of the U.S. Army's Department of the Pacific, came into direct conflict with Governor Stevens by criticizing his policies and the conduct of his territorial volunteers. A bitter feud erupted between the two men when General Wool refused to allow army troops to escort Stevens from Fort Benton through hostile Indian territory.

Antagonism between the regular army and the territorial volunteers escalated. Wool advocated a return to a policing action rather than aggressive warfare, to prevent illegal settlement, maintain peace, and protect the rights of the Indians until Stevens's treaties were ratified. The secretary of war approved of Wool's policy.

Hostilities erupted again in the spring of 1856 when the Indians attacked the blockhouse at the Cascades, a critical location for moving troops and supplies along the Columbia. The uprisings spread to other locations. Reinforced by the territorial volunteers, forces led by Colonel George Wright stepped up the military campaign.

Wright's men cut the Indians off from their food resources and inflicted heavy casualties. The warriors' resistance was soon crushed, and a truce was declared. Several of the minor Yakima leaders were hanged as examples.

The uneasy truce was short-lived. Non-Indian settlement of Indian lands continued in the Walla Walla Valley, provoking more uprisings. Regular army troops under the command of Major Robert S. Garnett were sent out to secure the Yakima sector. In order to control the Yakima Valley effectively and to keep trespassers and settlers out, Garnett ordered the construction of an army fort in the heart of Yakima country. By the fall of 1856, troops were occupying this garrison, which was named Fort Simcoe.

Meanwhile, Governor Stevens sent a group of mounted volunteers under the command of Lieutenant Colonel Benjamin F. Shaw to the Grande Ronde Valley in Oregon Territory. The expedition members began to battle Indians who had not been involved in the general fighting. Wool ordered Shaw out of the territory. After the summer of 1856, the volunteer forces were disbanded.

By the middle of September, the area east of the Cascades was once again at peace. Colonel Wright remained in command. Governor Stevens called for a second council at Fort Walla Walla, demanding unconditional surrender from the Indians. Remembering Peupeumoxmox's fate, Kamiakin,

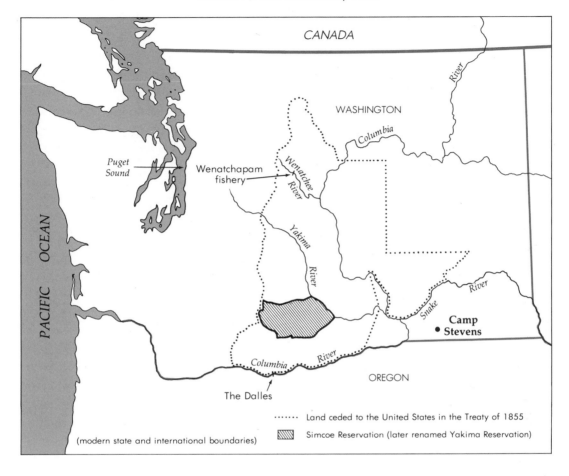

Owhi, and Qualchan refused to come. Kamiakin fled to stay with his Palus relatives.

Convinced that the interior Plateau lands were a natural homeland for Indians but unsuitable for white settlement, General Wool tried to resecure the area for the Indians. Demanding that all whites leave the area east of the Cascade Mountains, Wool closed the interior to white settlers by military order in 1857. The same year, Stevens re-signed his post as governor after he was elected as a delegate to Congress.

The region remained relatively peaceful until the summer of 1858, when gold was discovered on the Thompson and Fraser rivers in British Columbia, Canada. Once again prospectors illegally crossed Indian lands to reach the mining sites. And once again warfare broke out.

Colonel E. J. Steptoe was sent north from Fort Walla Walla to secure the area

An 1857 sketch of Fort Simcoe, which was built in the heart of Yakima country in 1856 to house regular army troops.

against an alliance of Yakima, Spokane, Palus, and Coeur d'Alene Indians. The army forces were defeated near present-day Rosario, Washington, and turned back. The Indian War of 1858 was fully launched, and soon the Nez Percé also joined the Indian alliance.

Major Garnett's forces were dispatched from Fort Simcoe to secure the Yakima territory, and Colonel Wright's men began to attack the Indian alliance near the Spokane River. Decisive battles were fought at Four Lakes and on the Spokane Plains. Wright's forces captured and killed 800 horses owned by Indians, and destroyed their cattle, grain, hay, and stored foods. Facing superior weaponry and lacking horses and supplies, the Indians were forced to retreat. Hostilities finally ended with the Indians' surrender on September 17, 1858. Priests of the Jesuit order who lived among the Coeur d'Alene helped to negotiate the terms of the peace between Wright and the Indians.

On September 23, Owhi turned himself in to Colonel Wright. The Yakima leader was arrested and ordered to send for his son Qualchan. When Qualchan rode into the army camp, he was seized and summarily hanged in the belief that he had killed Agent Bolon, a charge that was subsequently disproved. Owhi was later killed while trying to escape. Five Indians suspected of murdering the trespassing miners were also executed by Garnett's forces. Skloom, another of the treaty chiefs of the Yakima, never regained his lost prestige and died in 1861.

Understandably, Kamiakin refused to present himself to Wright. Although he had been injured in battle, he was able to flee to safety in Canada. Kamiakin continued to live in exile until his death at age 73 in 1877. Although the place of his burial was kept secret by his relatives, several years later vandals discovered the leader's grave and removed Kamiakin's head. It has never been recovered.

Wright himself paid a price for his role in the fighting. Despite his decisive victory over the Indian alliance, Wright was later assigned to a minor post. His continued defense of Indian rights was obviously not a popular or safe political position to take. General Wool, too, was eventually removed from his command.

The Yakima Treaty of 1855 was finally ratified by Congress on March 8, 1859. Four years after white settlers had begun to flood into the interior Plateau, the region was officially opened to settlement by non-Indians. The Yakima's battles had ended, but the peace had cost the Yakima Nation its most experienced and respected leaders. In this uneasy position, the Indians began to settle on their reservation and create a new life there. ▲

Yakima Indians performing a war dance on the Fourth of July, 1893.

ON THE
RESERVATION

As the Yakima continued to resettle on their reservation in the early 1860s, the U.S. Army troops stationed at Fort Simcoe withdrew from the post. The Bureau of Indian Affairs then took control of the buildings of the fort, which became the new Yakima Indian Agency. The army had built a wagon road along an Indian trail between Fort Simcoe and Fort Dalles on the Columbia River. This road would allow agents stationed there to have easier contact with government posts to the south.

Richard H. Lansdale was the first agent to take up residence at the Simcoe Agency. In 1860, Agent Lansdale tried to persuade Kamiakin to return to the reservation to become head chief of the new Yakima Indian Nation. Dispirited over the Yakima's loss of their lands and autonomy, Kamiakin refused. Spencer of the Klikitats was appointed head chief instead and served a short term. Following the reservation's first election in 1867, Joe Stwire, or White Swan, another Klikitat, became head chief. He served in this position until he died in 1910.

The person who was to have the greatest influence over the Yakima during the early reservation era was Reverend James H. Wilbur, who was called Father Wilbur by the people. Wilbur, a Methodist minister, came to Yakima territory in 1861 to be the first instructor of the newly founded Simcoe Agency boarding school. The founding of the institution, which initially enrolled 15

Indian boys and 3 girls, marked the start of formal education for reservation youngsters. Students there went to the school for half a day to learn to speak, read, and write the English language. The rest of the day they spent working on the school's farm. As the school grew, Wilbur was given the title of superintendent.

While holding this position, Wilbur became angered at the way the agency was being run. He complained directly to President Lincoln in Washington, D.C., that Agent Lansdale had reduced the Indians' annuity distributions to such an extent that local tribal leaders reported "they were not worth making the trip to secure." Lincoln responded by appointing Wilbur the tribe's new agent in 1865.

As agent, Wilbur worked tirelessly to develop the reservation assets. He encouraged the Indians to farm and to continue raising cattle and other livestock. The minister also established the first tribally owned cattle herds, but unfortunately he used funds that the government had allocated to the Yakima for blankets and clothing. In addition, Wilbur expanded an irrigation project that had been started in 1860 near Ahtanum, where Kamiakin had dug his irrigation ditch to water his gardens 20 years earlier. By 1865, between 1,000 and 1,200 acres of tribal lands were irrigated. Wilbur also reported that four to six homes were being built each year to replace mat lodges.

Other changes were taking place in the Yakima Valley. Between 1860 and 1861, the first white family settled just northeast of the reservation. They were rapidly followed by other non-Indian homesteaders. In 1866, a stagecoach road through the reservation was opened. (The present-day U.S. Highway 97 closely parallels this route.) The outside world was beginning to encroach on the reservation. By 1872, non-Indian families were also using water from Ahtanum Creek to cultivate their fields, a practice that was shortly to become competitive with Indian use.

In 1867, Father Louis Napoleon St. Onge was sent by the Catholic Oblates to rebuild St. Joseph's Mission on Ahtanum Creek. Using the grammar and dictionary of the Yakima language published by Father Pandosy in 1862, St. Onge devised a Yakima alphabet and translated a catechism and Catholic prayers into the Indians' own tongue. (This was the first time the language appeared in written form.) As the Oblates increased their efforts to convert the Yakima, a bitter rivalry developed between the Methodist and Catholic missionaries on the reservation. In 1871, Wilbur once again traveled to Washington, D.C., and met with President Ulysses S. Grant. He persuaded the president to place the Yakima reservation in the care of the Methodist church. Thereafter, Catholic missionaries were banished from the reservation. However, Jesuit priests then established a church and boarding school in the town of North Yakima, just outside the northern boundaries of the reservation. Many of the Yakima who had previously been converted to Catholicism began to attend services here and enroll their children in the school.

In the late 19th century, the Yakima's agricultural development continued to increase. By 1871, the Yakima had 3,000 acres under cultivation and 4,000 acres fenced. They owned an estimated 10,000 to 12,000 horses and 1,400 head of cattle. The horses alone were worth $195,000. By 1878, the number of cattle increased to 3,500 head, and the horse herd had grown to 16,000. The people were also cutting timber and catching a large number of salmon to sell.

Throughout this expansion in ranching and farming, the majority of Yakima continued to rely for their livelihood on fishing, gathering, and hunting. Wilbur reported to the commissioner of Indian affairs that only slightly more than one-fourth of the Yakima population had become "civilized" farmers.

Controversy still exists over the tactics Wilbur used to "civilize" the Indians. He was described as a strict disciplinarian whose law was "no work, no food." Indians who farmed were given teams of horses, wagons, plows, harrows, harnesses, rations of beef, clothing, and other valuable goods that the government sent to the reservation as part of its treaty obligations. Wilbur was further accused of favoring those Indians who converted to Methodism. Some converts were said to attend church services just to be cer-

Reverend James H. Wilbur, who President Abraham Lincoln appointed the Yakima's agent in 1865.

tain to receive preferential treatment from the agent. The Indians also complained that Wilbur tried to enforce hair cutting and refused to give annuities to those who followed "longhair" Indian religious practices. But in spite of Wilbur's coercive tactics, traditional Yakima beliefs and customs persisted, in particular the Wáashat, or the Indian longhouse religion.

The principal center for Wáashat services among the Yakima between 1870 and 1890 was the longhouse of Kotiahkan at Pá?xotakyut, the site of an extensive aboriginal village where the present-day town of Parker, Washington, is located. Kotiahkan was a son of Showaway, one of the brothers of the great Yakima chief Kamiakin. James Mooney, an early ethnographer in the area, recorded in the late 1880s that regular Wáashat services took place on Sunday—which the Yakima called "the great 'medicine day' of the whites"—in the morning, afternoon, and evening. Services were also held during the week and for "special periodic observances, such as the 'lament' for the dead, particularly the dead chiefs, in the early spring; the salmon dance, when the salmon begin to run in April; and the berry dance, when the wild berries ripen in autumn."

Two events of significance that would pose a particular threat to the traditional Yakima way of life took place in the 1880s: the completion of the Northern Pacific Railroad and the passage of the Indian Homestead Act. The Northern Pacific Railroad began operating along the Yakima River valley in 1883. This opened a direct line to outside markets for products raised in the valley and provided a major stimulus

A 19th-century engraving of Indians watching a train of the Northern Pacific Railroad. The railroad brought a huge number of non-Indians to the Yakima River valley in the late 1800s.

for development. The area surrounding the reservation soon saw rapid increases in white settlement. The Yakima complained to the government about the influx, and in 1884 Major J. W. MacMurray was sent to the reservation by the Department of the Pacific to investigate the problem. MacMurray reported that the main railroad tracks were routed right through the richest and most heavily populated areas of the Indians' lands, including their fields and orchards. In addition, extensive homesteading on land adjacent to the reservation had led to mounting legal disputes between the Yakima and non-Indians over who had the right to the water and fish in nearby waterways.

In the same year, the Indian Homestead Act extended the Homestead Act of 1862 to Indians. Under the terms of the 1862 legislation, any citizen over 21 was able to claim 160 acres of unoccupied government-owned land in an unsettled region of the country. The Indian Homestead Act, therefore, allowed Indians to obtain homesteads on public lands just as non-Indian Americans could. Like reservation territory, these homesteads were to be held in trust by the federal government and could not be taxed.

On his inspection tour, MacMurray found that the Yakima who had opted to take up lands under the Indian Homestead Act were being compelled by their current agent, R. H. Milroy, to return to the reservation. MacMurray reported that Milroy had asked the government to send troops to help him drive the Indians from their homesteads back to the reservation. Ironically, the Yakima themselves also telegraphed the military, requesting that soldiers be dispatched to their homesteads to protect them from the agency's Indian police force. In spite of the repressive actions of Milroy, Yakima families established about 100 homesteads on lands south of the reservation, many clustered along Rock Creek.

Among the many causes for the Yakima's complaints, MacMurray also cited the impact of the railroad, opposition of the agent to traditional Indian customs and beliefs, agency misuse of Indian funds, and the

interference by the Indian officials, at the Simcoe, or "Yakima Agency," with the domestic life of these people. . . . Many live in neat looking frame houses, have large fields, orchards and gardens, cattle and horses, pigs, goats and sheep. The majority, however, do not live in civilized houses; but keep to the old Indian style of architecture, a large framework of posts and poles, covered with a rush matting, which they are skilled in making, although they often have fields and barns, and excellent orchards.

The Indians were obviously making choices, selecting what to adopt from white culture and what to retain from their own.

Despite the Yakima's many difficulties, they were prospering on the reservation. Although many non-Indians had settled just outside its boundaries, their land had largely remained closed to outsiders, and the reservation's resources were being used to benefit the Yakima people. The reservation had its own police force and court to hear cases involving its inhabitants. The Yakima also had schools, irrigation systems, logging and milling operations, and even a wage-earning work force. They were increasing their agricultural production and home and road construction as well. The Yakima had been able to guard their rights.

But this was not to last for long. In the final decades of the 19th century, the American public applied great pressure on the government to open all lands—including the Indian reservations—to private ownership. Congress responded by passing the General Allotment Act of 1887. This legislation would bring about profound problems for the Yakima Indian Nation.

The General Allotment Act, also known as the Dawes Act, canceled many of the guarantees the government had made in its treaties with Indian groups throughout the United States. Reservation lands were no longer to be held in common by tribes and used by Indians exclusively. The act authorized the division of reservations into tracts (or allotments) of 80 acres of farmland or 160 acres of grazing or timber land. Each tribal member

would then receive one allotment as his or her private property. The land could not be sold for 25 years, the time the government deemed that Indians would need to blend into mainstream American society. After this period, allottees would be issued a fee patent, giving the landowners clear title to do whatever they wished with their tracts. Subsequent amendments to the act permitted Indians to lease their allotments, sell land they had inherited, or in some cases receive a fee patent before the 25-year period had ended.

The Dawes Act also empowered the president to negotiate with tribes for purchase of "surplus lands"—that is, any territory left over after all members of a tribe on a reservation had received allotments. The government planned to resell the surplus to non-Indian settlers. The sales' proceeds would be used for Indian education and other "civilizing" benefits.

The Dawes Act's supporters hoped that it would help Indians assimilate into American culture. They reasoned that once the unallotted portions of reservations were opened to whites, the Indians' new neighbors could exert a "civilizing" influence on them. The government could then terminate all reservations and stop providing Indians with the special services promised in its treaties with the tribes. The "Indian problem," as well as the Indian, would disappear.

Ironically, the act's supporters ignored the past statements of perceptive military officers, agents, and the Indians themselves. These had made clear that many of the Indians' problems—such as prostitution, venereal disease, drunkenness, and poverty—were directly associated with their contact with whites at towns or trading centers. The very people who were supposed to make the Indians "civilized" Americans were causing their greatest miseries.

The Yakima themselves were split over the issue of allotment. Those who farmed—the "civilized" Indians—were in favor of dividing the reservation into privately owned parcels. But those who used large tracts of tribal land for grazing horses and cattle opposed the idea.

This position was also supported by the so-called wild Indians, the traditional "longhairs" who did not believe that land should be privately owned by individuals. The majority of Yakima Indians were reluctant to accept allotments.

Many also opposed the government's plan to purchase their unallotted reservation lands. In 1894, Special Inspector P. McCormick met with a group of the "wild and untamed" Yakima in Kotiahkan's tule mat longhouse, which had been moved just outside the reservation boundaries to avoid confrontation with the Yakima agent. McCormick later reported that the Yak-

Yakima children playing outside the school at the Simcoe Agency in 1916.

Two Yakima couples in traditional dress, photographed in the 1890s. Whites called traditionalists "longhairs" because they refused to cut their hair in the style of non-Indians.

ima told him, "We will not give up these lands." Several years later, Kotiahkan, aided by an interpreter, led a Yakima delegation to Washington, D.C., to fight the purchase of the Yakima's surplus reservation lands. The delegation's battle was successful. The Yakima Nation was allowed to retain its large tracts of unallotted timber and grazing lands.

The Yakima's fight against allotment of reservation land failed, however. To enforce its policy, the government informed all resisters that if they did not claim their allotments, the land would be opened to non-Indian homesteaders. Eventually most Yakima reluctantly accepted allotments.

As the Yakima were assigned tracts and issued fee patents, non-Indians began to infiltrate their land. Many promoted fraudulent land deals, often with the assistance of bootleg whiskey. The Indians' rights were ignored, and Indian-white relations worsened.

At this time, the Yakima were introduced to two Indian curing cults: the Indian Shakers and the Feather Cult. The Indian Shakers' religion spread from the Puget Sound area to the Columbia Plateau in 1899. It combines traditional Indian doctoring with Catholic and fundamentalist Christian doctrines. It is still popular on the Yakima Reservation. Two Shaker churches are located near White Swan and one near Satus. Members with the "shake," the power to cure, perform the cult's group rituals in private homes. Like traditional Indian doctors, they try to cure illnesses caused by supernatural powers and to remove threats from dangerous spiritual forces.

The Feather Cult was a curing religion founded by the Klikitat in about 1904. Its curing rituals were also performed in homes and focused primarily on helping people with drinking problems. Members of the Feather Cult also belonged to Wáashat, the Indian longhouse religion.

As allotment continued, Yakima country soon became like a checkerboard, as non-Indians established holdings among the Indian-owned allotments. First came white farmers and cattlemen, and then white traders. By the early 1900s, Oriental settlers arrived to start fruit orchards. Finally, Mexican-American migrants moved to the area to work as fruit pickers and farmhands.

Lucullus McWhorter, one of the few defenders of Indian rights at this time, wrote in 1913 that "practically all of the agriculturally productive land on the reservation was occupied by whites, either through leases or through sale or allotments." Valuable irrigation areas had gone out of Indian hands especially quickly. Reservation towns, such as Toppenish and Wapato, were founded during this period through purchases of fee patent land from Indian owners. Stimulated by the railroad, these new towns grew rapidly. Many Indians became day laborers, picking crops, freighting, and performing other types of seasonal work. The reservation was irrevocably opened.

By 1914, when the allotment of the Yakima Reservation ended, 4,506 tribal members had received a total of 440,000 acres, leaving 780,000 acres still tribally owned. Today, non-Indians own about 253,280 acres, more than half of the Indian land originally allotted. This land was principally in the lush irrigated lands on the eastern side of the reservation.

Tribal holdings increased, however. In 1900, the Yakima convinced the government to resurvey the reservation's western boundary. They had long maintained that the boundary was set farther east than it should have been according to the provisions of the 1855 treaty that established the reservation. After the survey, the boundary was redrawn farther west, adding 357,879 acres to the reservation. Through land purchases and other land returns, the Yakima Nation now communally owns 866,445 acres. In addition, Yakima individuals own approximately 260,000 acres. Most of the Yakima-owned territory is rich timberland and dry foothills good for stock grazing.

With the opening of the reservation, many existing problems escalated. Large-scale irrigation projects were developed both on and bordering the reservation. Political and legal battles quickly raged over who had the rights to the irrigation water. The irrigation projects drew water to off-reservation lands, diminishing the supply that was needed for reservation irrigation and for the Indians' livestock.

Irrigation dams prevented salmon from making their regular spawning runs, prompting more controversies involving fishing rights. In addition, small salmon, or fingerlings, were often caught in lateral irrigation canals. Unable to reach the rivers, they perished by the millions. In 1955, the Yakima tribal council reported that by the beginning of the 20th century the fish runs were becoming "critically depleted through irrigation . . . especially [on] the Yakima River" and that fishing villages had become "memories of the

past." White fisherman on the Columbia River added to the problem by using fish wheels. This method of fishing greatly depleted the fish runs.

The Yakima's right to fish at their traditional sites was also threatened. White homesteaders on lands adjoining the fisheries sometimes refused to allow the Indians to cross their lands in order to reach these stations. In 1905, the U.S. Supreme Court upheld the Indians' right to use their ancient and accustomed fisheries in *U.S. v. Winans*, a case brought against a white settler whose homestead blocked Indian access to these sites. The Court also ruled that the treaties the Indians had made with the U.S. government were to be interpreted the way the Indians had understood them. It stated that "a treaty was *not* a grant of rights *to* Indians but a grant of rights *from* them."

However, non-Indian fishermen often ignored the ruling. Eight years later, U.S. Attorney Francis Garrecht was called to defend Yakima Indian fishing rights in *U.S. v. the State of Washington*, a case involving two principal Yakima chiefs, George Meninock and Jim Wallahee. Meninock presented a moving speech as part of the trial testimony:

> God created this Indian country and it was like He spread out a big blanket. He put the Indians on it. . . . Then God created the fish in this river and put deer in these mountains and made laws through which has come

Two Yakima laborers employed as hop pickers by a white farmer (center) in Yakima Valley in the late 19th century.

Chief Sluiskias and his family pose outside their non-Indian-style home on the Yakima reservation in 1915.

the increase of fish and game. . . . For the women God made roots and berries to gather, and the Indians grew and multiplied as a people. When we were created we were given our ground to live on, and from that time these were our rights. This is all true. We had the fish before the missionaries came, before the white man came. . . . This was the food on which we lived. . . . My strength is from the fish; my blood is from the fish, from the roots and berries. The fish and the game are the essence of my life. . . . We never thought we would be troubled about these things, and I tell my people, and I believe it, it is not wrong for us to get this food. Whenever the seasons open, I raise my heart in thanks to the Creator for his bounty that this food has come.

Through the years, the Yakima Indian Nation was fairly successful in defending its treaty rights in the federal courts, but the abuses against them continued. For instance, the Yakima's traditional Indian fishing grounds at the Long Narrows and Great Cascades were flooded in 1938 when the U.S. government constructed Bonneville Dam on the Columbia River. Congress passed legislation promising that the salmon and steelhead that had been destroyed would be replaced by hatchery fish. However, this act was implemented by establishing almost all of the hatcheries downriver from Bonneville Dam, where only non-Indians fished, instead of upriver in the tribal fishing areas. Similar problems arose in 1941 when Grand Coulee Dam was built on the Columbia and blocked miles of spawning grounds.

The late 19th and early 20th centuries brought the Yakima into conflict with both white settlers and government officials as the tribe tried to hold on to the land and resources that were legally theirs. These years were only a prelude to the battles the Yakima Nation would be forced to fight in the last decades of the 20th century. ▲

Three-year-old Yakima William Reed, first-place winner in a tiny-tot dance competition at a powwow in Arleen, Montana, in 1985.

THE
YAKIMA NATION
TODAY

A visitor to the Yakima Indian Reservation today usually arrives on U.S. Highway 97, which runs north and south along part of its eastern boundary. A kaleidoscope of images emerges along the roadway: concession stands, fruit orchards, patches of sagebrush flats, motels, mobile homes, irrigation ditches, truck stops, small dwellings of clapboard siding, and periodic glimpses of snowcapped Mount Adams towering above the Cascades to the west.

Four miles south of the town of Yakima, an earth-colored road sign marks the entrance to the reservation. On it is the Yakima's official logo: a large projectile point on which appear illustrations of Mount Adams and an eagle carrying a banner reading Yakima Nation. Fourteen 5-pointed stars—representing the 14 "Confederate Tribes and

Bands" that came to live on the reservation—form a border around these images. In symbols, the logo helps to tell outsiders something about the heritage and history of the Yakima people.

There are, however, portions of their past and present that the Yakima prefer to keep more private. Most of the reservation to the west is seldom seen by the public. The region beyond Fort Simcoe is largely restricted, set aside for Yakima Indian use. Other people must obtain a special permit to gain entrance. A system of roads leads through this area to the Yakima's ancient root and berry grounds, hunting areas, and rangelands where their wild horse herds once roamed.

The Yakima Indian Agency, which was moved from Fort Simcoe to a location just west of the town of Toppenish in 1922, today remains the headquarters for tribal activities. Here, representatives of the Yakima people and officials of the Bureau of Indian Affairs have worked for decades to ensure the tribe's survival in the 20th century.

The beginning of the Yakima tribal government as it operates today dates to 1933. In that year, the Yakima first began to elect 14 representatives to a tribal council. In general, two members were selected from seven districts that were traditionally centers of tribal activity. Voting was by a show of hands. The representatives were to serve for life unless they resigned or were removed from their post by consensus.

The Indian Reorganization Act (IRA), which was passed by Congress in 1934, established guidelines for tribes to create their own government and constitution. Disillusioned by their past dealings with the U.S. government, the Yakima chose not to reorganize their government under the IRA. Instead, in 1946, they began to formalize their tribal government by establishing official "rules and procedures" that would guide its actions. In the same year, the Yakima made rules for membership in the general council, which comprised all of the people eligible to vote in council elections. To qualify, a person had to be at least 18 years old and an enrolled member of the Yakima Nation. To be eligible for enrollment, a person had to have one-fourth ancestry in 1 of the nation's 14 original tribes or bands. In 1949, the Yakima Nation's official roll was begun. A steady growth in population has resulted in an increase in the number of people enrolled since then. Today, about 8,000 persons are officially members of the Yakima Nation. About 5,000 live on the reservation, sharing their lands with approximately 20,000 non-Indians.

In 1947, the general council voted to change the tenure of council members to a four-year term. In order to ensure the continuity of council business, elections for half of the council positions would be held every two years. The tribal council began to operate under these terms in 1948.

The general council determines tribal policy, rules, and procedures; the tribal council actually transacts the business of the tribe. An executive board consisting of a chairman, vice-chairman, and secretary elected from the tribal council helps perform its day-to-day operations.

To organize and manage all of the diverse interests of the Yakima Nation, the tribal council has designated eight separate committees to be responsible for various functions of the council. The committees are named: Timber, Grazing, and Overall Economic Development; Loan, Extension, Education, and Housing; Fish, Wildlife, and Law and Order; Roads, Irrigation, and Land; Legislative; Health, Employment, Welfare, Recreation, and Youth Activities; Enrollment; and Budget and Finance.

One of the tribal council's principal concerns is adding to the Yakima's land base. For more than 25 years, the Yakima Nation has attempted to keep intact

A meeting of the Yakima General Council, held near Toppenish, Washington, in January 1921.

or increase the tribe's holdings by purchasing land that was put up for sale by the heirs of original allottees. After years of litigation with the U.S. government, the Yakima in 1972 also received title to 21,008 acres of land that had been excluded from their reservation because of a survey error. The return of this land, which included sacred Mount Adams, prompted a great celebration. Today, the Yakima Indian Reservation extends over 1,371,918 acres. Approximately 1,120,000 acres are owned either by individual tribal members or by the tribe itself.

The Yakima Nation has also battled the government in court over fishing rights. In the 1950s, the Yakima Nation was awarded $15,019,640 as compensation for the loss of the Celilo Falls fishery. The fishery, which belonged to the Yakima according to their 1855 treaty, had been flooded by the construction of the Dalles Dam on the Columbia River. From the cash award, $6,313,920 was held in trust for the educational needs of enrolled minors. Funds were also disbursed to all enrolled adults, each of whom received $3,270. But the immediate benefits of the settlement were counteracted by the long-term effects of losing the fishery. Many Yakima fishermen lost their only means of support, and families no longer had an important subsistence resource. The flooding of the Celilo Falls fishery eventually accounted for a 45 percent increase in Yakima unemployment.

The Dalles Dam was only 1 of 19 dams the government had constructed

Colonel J. U. Moorhead of the U.S. Army Corps of Engineers looks on as Yakima leader Kiu-tus Jim signs the tribe's 1954 Celilo Falls agreement with the federal government. The United States awarded the Yakima more than $15 million in compensation when this traditional fishing site was flooded by the construction of the Dalles Dam.

by 1975 on the Columbia and Snake rivers to harness hydroelectric power. Because they did not have adequate fish ladders—steplike structures built to help fish swim past dams—these dams have been responsible for the death of millions of salmon fingerlings. Low water levels during the peak of the irrigation season in the Yakima Valley also kill many smolts (young salmon).

Formerly, about 14 million salmon and steelhead trout had returned annually to the Columbia River and its tributaries to spawn. By 1980, this number had dropped to 2.5 million, the lowest fish run in history.

Drawing heavily on recommendations made by the Columbia River Intertribal Fish Commission, a consortium of Plateau Indian tribes, Congress legislated a new fish and wildlife conservation program to increase the fish runs damaged by the hydroelectric dams. By 1984, the situation had begun to improve. Today, the size of the fish runs is still growing.

The Yakima Nation itself is taking a primary role in rebuilding the fish runs of steelhead trout, chinook, sockeye, and silver salmon in the Yakima River basin. Their enhancement project calls for the construction of a complex of hatcheries at Union Gap and other strategic sites at a cost of $25 million. This experimental hatchery complex will be the largest in the world. In addition, the Yakima have successfully lobbied for more than $50 million in federal government funds for building fish ladders and screens to prevent fingerlings from being trapped in irrigation ditches. Today, the Yakima Basin has been targeted to become one of the largest fishery conservation programs in the United States.

A closely related issue has been state regulation of off-reservation treaty fisheries. Conflicts regarding this regulation have repeatedly pitted the consortium of the Yakima, Umatilla, Warm Springs, and Nez Percé tribes against the state governments of Oregon and Washington. The right to take fish from these sites, which was granted to the Indians in their treaties with the U.S. government, has been recognized by two federal court decisions. In a 1969 case, *Sohappy v. Smith*, Judge Robert C. Belloni held that states were limited in their power to regulate Indian fisheries cited in these treaties and might do so only when necessary for conservation. In addition, the Belloni decision stated that regulations must not discriminate against Indians and that Indian fishermen were entitled to a "fair and equitable" share of the catch. In *U.S. v. Washington* in 1974, the ruling of Judge George Boldt held that a "fair and equitable" share was 50 percent of the harvestable fish swimming to "usual and accustomed" tribal fishing grounds and stations. The federal courts have also ruled that fishing at these sites is a tribal right, not an individual right, meaning that the authority to regulate tribal fishing on and off reservations is reserved for tribes. In spite of these decisions, state police in the Northwest continue to arrest individual Indian fishermen, and they are prosecuted in state courts. The state police's actions are supported by non-Indian sport and commercial fishermen who inaccurately cite "illegal" Indian fishing as the reason for the decline in the fish runs.

The issue of Yakima River water rights has also led to conflicts with the state of Washington. The Yakima Indian Nation, represented by the federal government, has been able to defend its water rights in the Yakima River basin because of the Yakima's legal primacy as "first users." Protection of their extensive irrigation system, fisheries, and other water uses remain at stake. A proclamation signed by the governor of Washington that formalized the "cooperative relationship" between the state administration and Indian tribes recognized by the federal government holds the promise of far fewer conflicts to arise in the future.

The Yakima Nation has also been successful in helping to avert the creation of a permanent storage facility for nuclear power plant wastes on the Hanford Nuclear Reservation. The proposed site was located to the east of the reservation on lands that the tribe had formerly ceded to the United States. When Hanford was named as one of the final possible sites for location of the facility, the Yakima established a Nuclear Waste Studies Program. Along with other groups, they expressed their concerns to the government about the repository's potential ill effects on tribal interests, including the risks to natural resources and sacred sites still used by the Yakima people. This concerted effort persuaded the government to choose another site.

The economic development of the reservation continues to be one of the tribal council's highest priorities. The largest industry within the reservation's boundaries is logging. Ninety percent of the tribe's annual income

comes from the timber in the closed area on the slopes of the Cascades. There the forest covers 600,000 acres, the largest stand of commercial timber on any Indian reservation in the United States. This valuable resource is carefully managed by the Yakima. No clear cutting—a common lumbering procedure that destroys the forests—is permitted. The tribe also derives income from selling hunting and fishing permits to outsiders and from leasing tribally owned farming and grazing lands.

In order to expand job opportunities for the Yakima people, the tribe has tried to develop other business enterprises. An industrial park has been established in the Wapato-Parker area. The largest tribally owned industry there is the Mount Adams Furniture Factory, which began operation in 1973. The factory produces quality furniture that is sold throughout the country. Most of the workers are of Indian descent and trained by tribal members. Some Yakima hold jobs in sawmills on or near the reservation. Others are employed by the Yakima Agency or are being trained as professionals for work in programs to improve the reservation's health and educational services. Indian personnel are playing an increasingly important role at the recently established substance abuse treatment center and in public and tribal schools. The Tribal Housing Authority also oversees a program to help low income families obtain better housing.

In spite of these efforts, low income and unemployment remain a problem.

Some Yakima families depend exclusively on money they receive by leasing their land for farming or grazing. Yet most must supplement their income by part-time or seasonal employment. The Yakima's traditional means of obtaining their livelihood has largely given way to the more sedentary life of wage work, but many people continue to rely on natural resources to augment their low income by hunting for venison and wild duck, fishing for trout and salmon, and gathering berries and roots.

Yakima Law and Order, the tribal police force and courts, has its own code of laws and law enforcement program. The tribal police patrol the boundaries of restricted areas, supervise encampments during celebrations, and enforce game and fish laws. The Yakima also have a tribal court to handle criminal offenses committed by In-

dians and hear civil suits between Indians and non-Indians when requested by both parties.

The Yakima Nation Review, the tribal newspaper, has been published since 1970. Issues now appear twice a month. The *Review* has become one of the most outstanding tribal newspapers in the country.

In 1922, when the Yakima Agency was moved to its present location, the agency boarding school was closed. Since that time, Yakima Indian children have either gone to off-reservation BIA boarding schools or have attended local public schools. Washington State's public school system is now contracted by the tribal council to run grade schools on the reservation.

One unique school—a tribally run institution called the Stanley Smartlowit Education Center after a tribal

Yakima men fishing from platforms at Parker Dam, 1965.

THE YAKIMA INDIAN RESERVATION TODAY

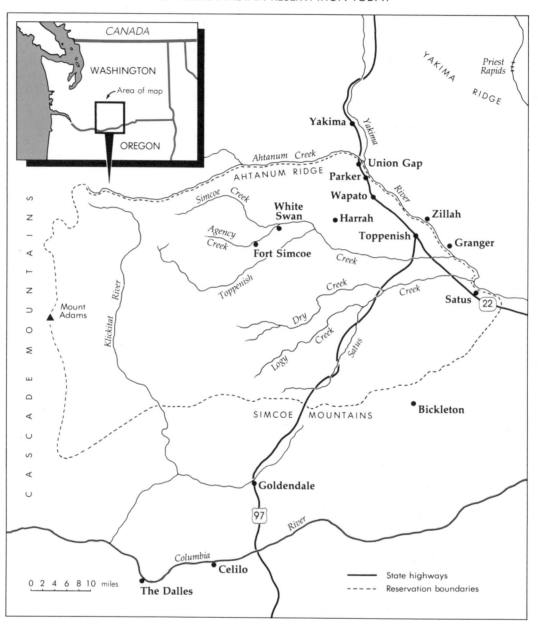

CANADA

WASHINGTON

Area of map

OREGON

YAKIMA RIDGE

Priest Rapids

Yakima

Union Gap

Ahtanum Creek

AHTANUM RIDGE

Parker

Simcoe Creek

Wapato

Zillah

White Swan

Harrah

Toppenish

Granger

Agency Creek

Fort Simcoe

Creek

Klickitat River

Toppenish Creek

Creek

Creek

Satus

22

Mount Adams

Dry Creek

Logy Creek

Satus Creek

Bickleton

SIMCOE MOUNTAINS

CASCADE MOUNTAINS

Goldendale

97

River

Columbia

Celilo

0 2 4 6 8 10 miles

The Dalles

———— State highways

- - - - Reservation boundaries

leader who did much to promote education on the reservation—is also available to Yakima children. A major change has taken place in the curriculums of reservation public schools since the 1960s. The Yakima language is now taught in the public school system and in adult education classes. Innovative programs are also used to teach children about Yakima culture and heritage. For instance, students participate in sacred first-foods feasts while sitting on tule mats in a longhouse. Other programs have been developed that reenact ancient legends and perform tribal dances for schoolchildren.

Some Yakima youngsters who come from homes where English is a second language find themselves at a disadvantage in a predominantly white-run school system. To improve basic skills in speaking, reading, writing, and mathematics, Indian students in grades three through nine can attend an educational summer facility called Camp Chaparral, located in the wooded foothills of Mount Adams. One of the camp's major goals is to build Indian youngsters' confidence and increase their desire to go on to higher education. The Yakima language is also taught so that the children can communicate in two cultures. During field trips on the mountain slopes, scientific explanations of natural phenomena are complemented by mythical tales told around evening campfires.

The Yakima people are extremely proud of their Cultural Heritage Center,

which opened in June 1980. The center was built not only to preserve the Yakima's treasured heritage but also to provide a place where they could share it with others. The Cultural Heritage Center consists of several buildings. In the middle of this complex, towering 76 feet above the sagebrush plains, is an imposing winter lodge—a community hall for meetings, banquets, special tribal programs, and conventions. The winter lodge has been designed as a modern version of the ancient mat lodge or longhouse. The center's Heritage Inn Restaurant features Indian foods. Customers can dine on buffalo steaks, Columbia River salmon, Indian fried bread, and homemade huckleberry pie. The heart of the center is a museum that features exhibitions that are planned, designed, and built principally by Yakima museum personnel. A visitor is guided through the exhibitions by plaques printed with stories narrated by Speelyáy. These ancient stories tell of the life of the Yakima people since they were first created on the land they still call home.

The Cultural Heritage Center is also the home of a library that specializes in books on American Indians and a shop that sells published material about various Plateau groups. Locally made beaded buckskin articles, pottery, and basketry can also be purchased there.

There has been a renewed interest in basketmaking on the Yakima Reservation. Many older women have begun to teach younger women and girls to weave baskets using traditional methods. Conservative families still use baskets for storing roots and picking berries, and offer them as gifts during giveaways and during trades between families on ceremonial occasions. Modern Yakima families also highly value fine baskets. They often place them on display in their homes as beautiful, prized heirlooms.

Today, the Yakima Indians' approach to health and illness is pragmatic. Certain illnesses are recognized as "white men's diseases." People ill with these go to the Yakima Nation Health Center at the Yakima Agency or to other medical facilities, where they are treated by doctors who practice modern medicine. The Yakima are now familiar with prescription medicines and with standard drugstore items, such as aspirin, but they still value their knowledge of the medicinal properties of native plants. For those illnesses that

The Yakima Cultural Heritage Center, which opened in June 1980, hosts special tribal programs, feasts, and dances.

may be treated with Indian curing methods, the Yakima avail themselves of an Indian Shaker curing rite or perhaps the services of a respected Indian medicine doctor. The traditional and modern coexist with little friction.

Wáashat services have changed little. However, the dress of worshipers has altered slightly in modern times. Women still wear moccasins, but they now dress in shawls and *k'lpíp*, a cotton version of the traditional buckskin dress. Men are outfitted in moccasins and beaded vests and usually trousers made of cloth. Men's hair, once worn long and loose, is now braided and often wrapped with otter fur. Face painting is no longer practiced.

The reservation longhouses still serve as the center of Yakima Indian culture, keeping alive the sentiments and values of a living Indian tradition. In recent times, longhouses have come to be used for purposes other than Wáashat services. It is now customary to hold family celebrations, wedding trades, and marriage ceremonies in these buildings.

There were three longhouses on the Yakima Reservation in the 1970s—one south of White Swan at the Toppenish Creek campgrounds, one just outside the town of Wapato, and one at Satus. The Toppenish Creek longhouse has since been torn down; a replacement is being built.

The basic plan of the old Toppenish Creek longhouse was characteristic of that of most modern longhouses. After entering its doorway, which was on the east side of the building, one would find a rectangular hall approximately 150 feet long and 40 feet wide. Storerooms were located to the right and a kitchen and long dining room to the left. The sides of the floor surrounding the ritual dance area, where the congregation and ritual specialists sat, were covered with a cement surface and carpeted. A long, narrow dance area with a hard-packed earthen floor was in the center of the hall. The walls of the room were cement block, and the gabled ceiling was crossed by rafters, studs, and crossbeams. Two open holes in the ceiling, one at each end, were reminiscent of the smokestacks that longhouses had when they were heated by stoves. Long poles were suspended horizontally from the lower rafters and used for hanging clothing and other paraphernalia on occasions when people might stay in a longhouse overnight. Nails on each side of the rounded western end of the hall held the ceremonial drums. Heat lamps were also hung nearby so that the drumheads could be kept warm and thus have the tension to produce tones and resonances properly. A long bench and several chairs for the bell ringer and drummers faced the center of the room on the western end.

The Yakima continue to maintain close ties to worshipers at longhouses at Priest Rapids on the Columbia River where the ancient Wanapam village of P'ná was located and at Simnasho on the Warm Springs Reservation in Oregon. The longhouse network also extends to those that have recently been rebuilt at Rock Creek, Celilo, and at Nespelem on the Colville Reservation in eastern Washington. But there is general agreement that the center of Wáashat activities is on the Yakima Reservation, where longhouse communities are more active than in any other part of the Columbia Plateau.

In a sense, Yakima Indian identity is represented by the longhouse itself. It is here, in the modern representation of the ancient extended family lodge, that the Yakima language, dress, foods, customs, values, and beliefs still exist. This is the wellspring of the Yakima people.

Today, longhouse Indian religious beliefs and practices coexist comfortably with Christianity. Many different Christian denominations are now represented in reservation churches, including Catholic, Methodist, Lutheran, Baptist, Presbyterian, Union Gospel, Disciples of Christ, and various fundamentalist sects. Indians may be Catholic or Methodist or belong to another Christian church and still attend, help, and participate in traditional Indian Wáashat ceremonies. At the White Swan longhouse, children annually perform a Christmas play, directed by a minister of the Church of Christ, for an audience of both Indians and whites. From the longhouse point of view, there is not just one true religion. As one Yakima elder has explained, "To believe is to have faith, and faith of any kind that promotes the welfare of the people is good."

The Yakima tradition of holding community celebrations throughout the year continues to this day on the reservation. Annual events include numerous powwows with dance contests, drum group competitions, craft exhibitions, Indian food booths, and Indian games; all-Indian rodeos; and the Indian Invitational Basketball Tournament. Yakima of all ages participate in various competitive events. Paalyút, the bone game, is still a great favorite and draws large crowds of players, bettors, and spectators.

The Toppenish Creek Indian Encampment and Pow-Wow—an annual 10-day encampment held each July at Toppenish Creek, south of White Swan—is one of the largest gatherings. As many as 3,000 Indian people from throughout the Northwest, Canada, and the Plains attend this celebration.

The popularity of today's many celebrations has been a major factor in maintaining intertribal friendships, just as it was in the past. People still look forward to sponsoring annual get-togethers where they can renew their social ties. In order to attend powwows, rodeos, and encampments throughout the West, people drive long distances. Men and women take particular pride in wearing their finest heirloom outfits of beaded buckskin and feathers and their beautiful, handmade "dance" outfits at these events.

Elders still contribute greatly to keeping the Yakima's social ties strong, especially those between members of

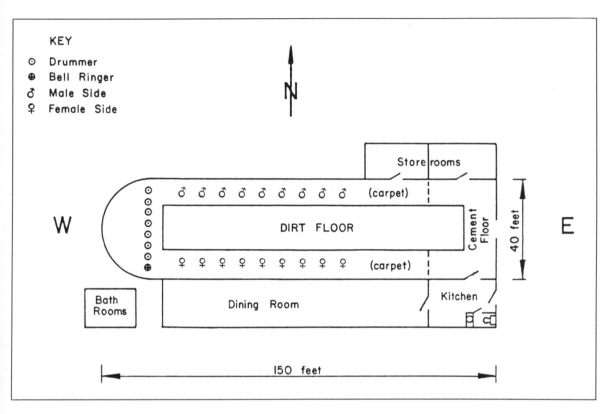

KEY
○ Drummer
⊕ Bell Ringer
♂ Male Side
♀ Female Side

N

W   E

Store rooms

♂ ♂ ♂ ♂ ♂ ♂ ♂ ♂ ♂   (carpet)

DIRT FLOOR

Cement Floor

40 feet

♀ ♀ ♀ ♀ ♀ ♀ ♀ ♀ ♀   (carpet)

Bath Rooms

Dining Room

Kitchen

150 feet

A plan of the interior of the Toppenish Creek longhouse, whose features are characteristic of most longhouses used for Wáashat services today.

extended families. A new generation of elders have now become longhouse leaders. They make certain that youngsters are still active participants in longhouse services and that ancient customs and beliefs are preserved. Older women often take groups of youngsters on root-digging expeditions. Elders also tell the stories of "long time" around evening campfires at Camp Chaparral. Some have become teachers' aides at public schools, where they instruct schoolchildren in the Yakima language.

As in ancient times, elders are still role models for Yakima youngsters.

Contemporary families tend to live in separate households. Traditional families in rural areas still try to live near close relatives, but each household no longer represents a true extended family. The Yakima are very much aware of these changes. They note that whereas they used to move together on horseback to root-digging and berry-gathering grounds, they now go separately in cars and trucks. "Now we live

Drummers waiting for the start of a dance at the annual rodeo in Ellensburg, Washington.

separate," they often say, with the sense that something is not quite right. Many Yakima miss the cooperation and sharing that "living together" promoted.

In spite of the many changes that the people have been forced to accept, they have managed to preserve much that is important from the past. And while they willingly avail themselves of formal education, desired conveniences, and important technologies that improve their health and living conditions, they maintain pride in their culture and in being part of the Yakima Nation. They are determined to preserve their remaining treaty rights in order to build a strong and secure future for the generations of Yakima yet unborn. A 1977 tribal booklet, *The Land of the Yakimas*, conveys these sentiments in a telling passage entitled "Retention of Customs and Beliefs," which accompanies a photograph of Mount Adams:

On a clear day "Páhto" [Mt. Adams], the sacred mountain of the Yakimas, towers above the Lower Yakima Valley. The great white mountain represents the ways of the past—the pursuit of game on the foothills, the gathering of wild plant foods on the lower slopes and the snows which give life to everything. Most of all, Mt. Adams symbolizes the strength of the Yakima people, who in spite of years of adversity, have forged a truly strong and great Nation. ▲

BIBLIOGRAPHY

Beavert, Virginia. *The Way It Was: Anaku Iwacha, Yakima Indian Legends.* Olympia: Franklin Press, 1974.

Brown, William Compton: *The Indian Side of the Story.* Spokane, WA: C. W. Hill, 1961.

Guie, H. Dean. *Bugles in the Valley: Garnett's Fort Simcoe.* Portland: Oregon Historical Society, 1977.

————.*Tribal Days of the Yakima.* Yakima, WA: Republic Publishing Co.: 1937.

Helland, Maurice. *They Knew Our Valley.* Yakima, WA: Printed by author, 1975.

Kirk, Ruth, and Richard D. Daugherty. *Exploring Washington Archaeology.* Seattle: University of Washington Press, 1978.

McWhorter, Lucullus V. *Tragedy of Wahk-Shum: Prelude to the Yakima Indian War, 1855–1856.* Fairfield WA: Ye Galleon Press, 1968.

Ruby, Robert H., and John A. Brown. *A Guide to the Indian Tribes of the Pacific Northwest.* Norman: University of Oklahoma Press, 1960.

Schuster, Helen H. *The Yakimas: A Critical Bibliography.* Bloomington: Indiana University Press, 1982.

Splawn, Andrew J. *Ka-Mi-Akin, The Last Hero of the Yakimas.* Yakima, WA: Caxton Printers, 1958.

THE YAKIMA AT A GLANCE

TRIBE *Yakima*

CULTURE AREA *Plateau*

GEOGRAPHY *Semiarid plateau region in Washington State, bisected by the Yakima River and its tributaries and bounded by the Cascade Mountains on the west and the Columbia River on the east.*

LINGUISTIC FAMILY *Sahaptian*

CURRENT POPULATION *Approximately 8,000*

FIRST CONTACT *Lewis and Clark Exploratory Expedition, American, 1805*

FEDERAL STATUS *The Consolidated Tribes and Bands of the Yakima Indian Nation is a federally recognized American Indian tribe with trust status. Its members live principally on the Yakima Indian Reservation, which extends more than 1,371,918 acres in south-central Washington State. A portion of the Yakima's traditional territory, this land was retained by them as a reservation according to the terms of the Treaty of 1855. Approximately 1,200,000 acres are owned either by individual tribal members or by the tribe itself.*

agent A person appointed by the commissioner of Indian affairs to supervise U.S. government programs and policies on a reservation and/or in a specific region. After 1908 the title *superintendent* replaced *agent*.

band A territorially based and simply organized group of people who are substantially dependent upon hunting and gathering for their subsistence.

Boldt Decision The 1974 ruling of federal court judge George H. Boldt, in *United States v. the State of Washington*. The decision stated that the U.S. government's past treaties with Indian groups in the Northwest ensure the right of their descendants to fish in "their usual and accustomed" tribal fishing sites. It also entitles these groups to catch up to half of all the fish in these areas.

Bureau of Indian Affairs (BIA) A U.S. government agency within the Department of the Interior. Originally intended to manage trade and other relations with Indians, the BIA now seeks to develop and implement programs that encourage Indians to manage their own affairs and to improve their educational opportunities and general social and economic well-being.

culture The learned and shared values, beliefs, and behavior of humans; nonbiological, socially taught activities; the way of life of a group of people.

dentalium shell A tubular white shell found only north of the Strait of Juan de Fuca in the Pacific Northwest. Known as haiqua, the shell traditionally was the standard medium of exchange for Northwest tribal peoples, including the Yakima.

dialect A regional variety of a language whose vocabulary, grammar, and pronunciation differ from other regional varieties. Together, these constitute a single language of which no one variety is construed as standard.

encampment Annual Yakima gathering, traditionally held at villages, camps, or special locations throughout the territory.

ethnographer A scholar who studies and systematically records information about a particular way of life of a society.

General Allotment Act An act passed by Congress in 1887 that provided for the division of Indian reservations into individually owned tracts of land. Allotment was intended as much to discourage traditional communal activities as to encourage the development of private farming and assimilate Indians into mainstream American life.

Indian Homestead Act An act passed by Congress in 1884 that permitted Indians to obtain homesteads on public domain lands, just as American citizens could according to the terms of the Homestead Act of 1862. Like reservation lands, Indians' homesteads were to be held in trust by the federal government and were not taxable.

Indian Reorganization Act (IRA) The 1934 federal law that ended the policy of allotting plots of land to individuals and provided for the political and economic development of reservation communities. The responsibilities of self-government were encouraged, and tribes wrote their own constitutions for that purpose.

linguist A scholar who specializes in the study of language.

longhouse Traditional Yakima lodge that usually housed an extended family, made up of grandparents, parents, and grandchildren. They evolved into traditional community structures.

missionary An advocate of a particular religion who tries to convert nonbelievers to his or her faith.

reservation A tract of land retained by Indians or set aside by the U.S. government for Indian occupation and use according to the terms of treaties negotiated between Indian groups and the United States.

Speelyáy A legendary character, also known as Coyote, in Yakima lore. A mischievous trickster and culture hero, Speelyáy concocted plans that sometimes greatly benefited the world. Other times his plans backfired, making him a victim of his own scheming.

tákh The Yakima word for a supernatural guardian spirit. As children, Yakima individuals obtained tákh, who gave their recipients special abilities and protected them throughout their life.

territory A defined region of the United States that is not, but may become, a state. The governor of a territory is appointed by the president, but territory residents elect their own legislature.

treaty A contract negotiated between representatives of the U.S. government or another national government and other recognized sovereign nations, including Indian tribes. Treaties dealt with the cessation of military action, maintenance of peace and friendship, the surrender of political independence, trade relationships, land cessions and the establishment of boundaries, U.S. government obligations, and related matters.

tribe A society consisting of several or many separate, fairly autonomous communities united by kinship, culture, language, and other social institutions.

twáti The highest rank of Yakima medicine doctors.

vision quest The ritual during which Yakima children spend time alone in a remote isolated setting, often in the mountains, in the hope of receiving a visit from a guardian spirit (tákh).

Wáashat A complex of traditional Yakima religious beliefs and practices also known as the longhouse, seven drum, or Indian religion. The Yakima consider this to be their native religion from time immemorial.

Yakima Nation A political and social entity formed according to the guidelines of an 1855 treaty with the U.S. government. The "nation" comprises 14 formerly independent bands or tribes that include the Yakima and many of their neighbors. Though previously independent of each other, these groups had all maintained close ties and alliances through marriage, the sharing of food and settlement sites, trade, and participation in intertribal gatherings.

INDEX

PICTURE CREDITS

HELEN H. SCHUSTER is associate professor of anthropology at Iowa State University. She holds B.A., M.A., and Ph.D. degrees in anthropology from the University of Washington in Seattle. She was awarded a postdoctoral research fellowship by the D'Arcy McNickle Center for the History of the American Indian at the Newberry Library and has received grants from the American Council of Learned Societies, the National Science Foundation, the Jacobs Foundation, the Wyoming Council on the Arts, and the National Endowment for the Humanities. Her book *The Yakimas: A Critical Bibliography* was selected as an Outstanding Academic Book for 1982 by *Choice*. Dr. Schuster has served on the board of directors of the Native American Art Studies Association and of the Council on Anthropology and Education.

FRANK W. PORTER III, general editor of INDIANS OF NORTH AMERICA, is director of the Chelsea House Foundation for American Indian Studies. He holds a B.A., M.A., and Ph.D. from the University of Maryland. He has done extensive research concerning the Indians of Maryland and Delaware and is the author of numerous articles on their history, archaeology, geography, and ethnography. He was formerly director of the Maryland Commission on Indian Affairs and American Indian Research and Resource Institute, Gettysburg, Pennsylvania, and he has received grants from the Delaware Humanities Forum, the Maryland Committee for the Humanities, the Ford Foundation, and the National Endowment for the Humanities, among others. Dr. Porter is the author of *The Bureau of Indian Affairs* in the Chelsea House KNOW YOUR GOVERNMENT series.